THE WORLD OF TREES

THE WORLD OF NATURE

THE WORLD OF TREES

HERBERT L. EDLIN and **MAURICE NIMMO**

with a foreword by **LORD SANDFORD**

BOUNTY BOOKS
A Division of Crown Publishers, Inc., New York

Contents

Foreword

Trees are one of the most magnificent forms of life to be found in the world. Among them are the largest and longest living of God's creatures. Until stone-age man began their destruction several thousand years ago, they were the most widespread type of vegetable life. They have been so important to man, as his uses for timber have multiplied, that many species are now in danger, and, like all the world's resources, the forests must now be husbanded with care.

In the British Isles, once almost completely covered by forests, there has been anxiety about the dwindling reserves of timber for over three hundred years. Now Britain has one of the smallest forest reserves of any country in Europe, when measured against the large population and the small land area. It is no wonder, then, that the trees of Britain are more cherished than ever before, and that 1973 was declared National Tree Planting Year. Nor is Britain an isolated case – all over the world people are becoming aware of the threat to this beautiful and valuable resource.

The trees that surround us are regarded in a great variety of ways. The timber merchant regards them, and the softwoods in particular, as a crop from which he wants the maximum financial return. The joiner and craftsman look to the more handsome hardwoods for the quality of the objects that can be made from them. The lover of the countryside enjoys trees for their adornment of the rural landscape. The upland farmer values woodlands for the shelter they afford his cattle, while the city dweller welcomes the relief, shade and beauty with which trees can offset the harshness and heat of asphalt and concrete.

Herbert Edlin and Maurice Nimmo transcend all such partial views. They invite us in this book to look through their sensitive and experienced eyes and to see trees as the noble creatures they are, full of beauty and dignity, so that we can learn to enjoy them for themselves. This book will, I believe, enchant the experienced forester as well as the city dweller. It will help to transform the casual acquaintance we all have with trees into a lasting familiarity and friendship.

LORD SANDFORD

Glossary

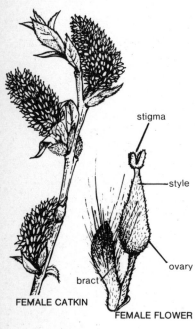

stigma

style

ovary

bract

FEMALE CATKIN

FEMALE FLOWER

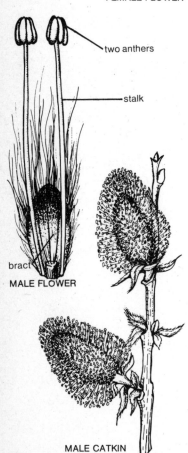

two anthers

stalk

bract

MALE FLOWER

MALE CATKIN

Annual ring Circular zone of timber formed by one year's outward growth of a woody stem. Contains an inner zone of *springwood* (q.v.) and an outer zone of *summerwood* (q.v.).

Anther Pollen-bearing organ at the tip of a stamen.

Auricle Ear-shaped extension at the base of a leaf.

Axil Upper angle between shoot and leaf, or leaf-stalk.

Bract Small, leaf-like structure borne on a stalk or in a flower of the *catkin* type (q.v.).

Bracteole A small bract, often found in catkin-type flowers.

Carpel Seed-bearing structure at the heart of a flower, usually joined with others in the *ovary* (q.v.), but distinct in certain species.

Catkin Clusters of simple flowers of one sex only (exception, sweet chestnut). Most are adapted to pollination entirely by wind (exceptions, sweet chestnut and willows).

Calyx All the *sepals* (q.v.), often fused as a tube. The calyx protects the flower while in bud.

Cotyledon See 'seed-leaf'.

Epiphytic Growing upon another plant, e.g. a fern rooted on an oak bough.

Graft Grafting implies the artificial union of a living shoot, or *scion*, from one tree, with the supporting rootstock, or *stock*, of another. The resulting tree is called a *graft*.

Heartwood Inner zone of a large woody stem, which has ceased to transport sap, and has, in most trees, become darker in colour. All heartwood is formed by chemical change from *sapwood* (q.v.).

Hybrid Offspring of parent trees of different species. The symbol × preceding the specific name indicates hybrid origin.

Layer Young tree propagated by bending down a side branch of an older tree and pegging it in the soil to take root.

Mid-rib Central stalk of a *pinnately* (q.v.) compound leaf, or central vein of an undivided leaf.

Nectary Organ found at the heart of many kinds of flowers, which secretes the nectar that attracts pollinating insects.

Ovary Part of a flower's female pistil. The ovary is situated at the base, and is made up of *carpels* (q.v.).

Palmate(ly) With lobes or leaflets radiating from a point.

Panicle Inflorescence with stalked flowers branching from a central stem.

Pedunculate Standing on a distinct stalk.

Petal Leaf-like structure, forming part of the corolla in many flowers and usually brightly coloured.

Pinnate(ly) With lobes or leaflets in series on both sides of a common stalk.

Pistil The complete female organ of a flower, comprising *ovary, style* and *stigma* (q.v.).

Pollard A tree that has been pollarded, i.e. cut back repeatedly at intervals of a few years to harvest crops of thin poles. It usually becomes swollen at the stem top.

Sapwood The whole substance of a small, young, woody stem, or the outer zone only of a larger, older one, which actively carries sap upwards. Usually paler than *heartwood* (q.v.).

Seed-leaf or **cotyledon** A leaf formed as part of a seed and enclosed within it. Cotyledons may emerge and function as green leaves or remain within the seed as a food store. Broadleaved trees have two seed-leaves; conifers from two to twenty.

Sepal A leaf-like structure forming part of the *calyx* (q.v.) of a typical flower, which it protects in the bud.

Sessile Borne directly on a main twig, with no individual stalk or peduncle.

Springwood Light, soft, pale wood, with much space to conduct sap upwards, formed in spring as the inner zone of an *annual ring* (q.v.).

Spur Short shoot arising from a longer shoot on certain trees, such as apples. Only the spurs bear flowers and fruit.

Stamen Male organ of a flower, bearing *anthers* (q.v.) that shed pollen.

Stigma Female organ at the tip of the *style* (q.v.) which receives pollen.

Style Part of a flower's female *pistil* (q.v.). The style links the *ovary* (q.v.) with the *stigma* (q.v.) and transports pollen to the ovary.

Sucker Young tree arising as a shoot from the root of an older one.

Summerwood Heavy, hard, strong and dark-coloured wood, with stout cell walls to give support, formed in summer as the outer zone of an *annual ring* (q.v.).

Transpiration Essential life process whereby trees take in water from the soil, through their roots, and let it escape later through their leaves.

Umbel A flower cluster in which the stalks of separate flowers radiate from a central point, like the ribs of an umbrella.

Umbo Rough, raised centre of a scale in the cone of certain conifers, particularly pines. In some conifers it bears a prickle.

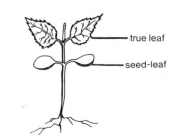

true leaf

seed-leaf

TYPICAL SEEDLING

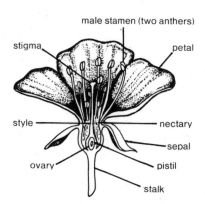

male stamen (two anthers)

stigma

petal

style

nectary

ovary

sepal

pistil

stalk

TYPICAL COMPLETE FLOWER

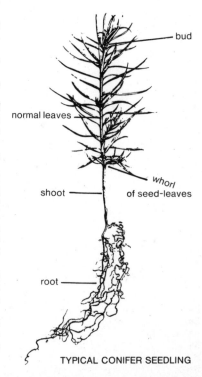

bud

normal leaves

shoot

whorl
of seed-leaves

root

TYPICAL CONIFER SEEDLING

Index of trees

Author's note on seasonal growth
The months quoted for leafing-out, flowering and fuiting relate, where appropriate, to a normal year in the lowlands of northern Europe, latitude 50 degrees, and to the north-eastern United States, latitude 42 degrees. Further north or in the uplands, as well as in years with exceptionally cold, late springs, seasonal growth may occur up to one month later. Further south, of course, it may be earlier.

The nature of trees

Below: In garden planning, only trees can give essential elements of shelter, colour, form and space. Here tall golden thujas frame pink rhododendrons, yellow azaleas and copper-foliaged dwarf maples, flanking green lawns

Trees enter into the lives of us all. They are the source of materials we need for many everyday purposes. They give shelter against wind and shade from the sun. Above all, they provide beauty in our outlook on the world. Larger than man, they endure for longer spans of years, and one can enjoy the attractions of a single well-loved tree through a whole lifetime. Yet it will always be changing, from the vigorous growth of its shapely youth until it reaches the rugged grandeur of its old age, when it reflects, in twisted boughs and wrinkled bark, struggles with the elements which have lasted for a hundred years and more.

The seasonal pattern of growth followed by all trees in temperate climates with warm summers and cooler winters is shown best by the deciduous broadleaved trees that lose their leaves each autumn. With them, every spring is clearly seen as a renewal of active life, through the development of fresh young elements. Encouraged by the warmth of April, the resting buds break out along every twig. Tender leaves expand their bright green blades to catch the sunshine, each taking on the elegant symmetrical shape peculiar to its kind. At the same time the shoots elongate to help form new twigs that will extend the tree's main stems and crown of foliage, in a pattern of regular or random growth peculiar to the trees of each particular kind. Unseen, but no less important, the root system is expanded below ground to supply the tree's growing trunk and foliage. Below the bark, cells divide adding a new zone of wood. Even the bark itself is expanding and gaining new characteristics, expressive of the kind of tree that it protects.

Throughout summer the crowns of expanded foliage display their varied wealth of restful greens. On some trees, like the birches, the crown is light and delicate, allowing much sunlight to filter through. Others, like the beeches, bear deep, dense crowns, so that the sunshine highlights their outer surfaces, but casts sombre shadows over the inner recesses.

As autumn approaches, the green pigments are withdrawn from the leaves, which now take on their underlying hues of yellow, brown, orange or red, varying with their species and with the progress of intricate colour chemistry. We enjoy a magnificent, though short-lived, display of gay, vivid colours – amber, russet, flame, chocolate or purple, grouped in shapely masses and often enlivened by the wind stirring the fading foliage. Then, with the first frosts, the stalks break from the twigs and the brightly tinted fragments fall to the forest floor where they make a fresh carpet of colour beneath our feet.

The handsome framework of the branches now stands revealed in all its symmetry, stretching out into the finer mesh of the smaller twigs. Each sort of tree has its own way of spreading its limbs and shoots so as to fill the largest space available to it. This makes it possible to name, for example, a beech or poplar simply by surveying their silhouettes from afar. As winter advances, snow may outline the bare grey branches, or sparkling white hoar frost may clothe even the finest twigs in a silver raiment. The winter gales are sure to stir the crowns, and as the great limbs sway before the winds they reveal their immense strength and resilience.

The march of the seasons is also shown by the broadleaved trees' patterns of flowering and fruiting. A few, notably alders and elms, bear clusters of small, simple flowers which lack petals. These flowers can be seen before the leaves open and often as early as February. This habit assists the wind in spreading the pollen through the bare crowns without resistance from leaves. Other broadleaved trees, such as oaks and beeches, expand catkins amid the young foliage in May. Others again, like crab apples, laburnums and horse chestnuts or buckeyes, present a bold display of white, yellow or pink blossoms in spring or summer, contrasting with the rich green of their foliage. The fruits that follow show surprising variety – acorns, walnuts, chestnuts, black fruits with stone-like seeds such as cherries, scarlet rowan berries, winged seeds as in maples, or the tiny grains, tufted with white hairs, of willow or poplar. All add variety to the appearance of the trees that bear them. Next spring you may search the soil around each tree for sprouting seedlings, elegant in form but often, in their early years, quite unlike their parent trees.

Though most conifers, other than larches, are evergreen and remain clad in leaves the whole year round, they too have an exciting spell of spring growth. In April and May the shoots of pine, spruce and silver fir shed their protective bud scales and expand rapidly. Their fresh, bright green needles, grouped near the branch tips, then make an effective, attractive contrast with the darker foliage that remains from previous years.

Conifer flowers, though often overlooked, are shapely and colourful structures. The males are usually a gay yellow and the females a pleasing pink or crimson. In autumn brown, woody cones add further character to the massed green foliage. In winter the conifers of northern countries are sure to become decked with snow. The snow outlines the curves of their strong branches, which can hold the weight unharmed.

Inevitably we associate trees with places where the scene is improved by their presence, so that they form an organic element of the landscape. The pines, firs and larches of the mountain foothills look exactly right when framed by their background of high, pointed peaks and craggy ridges, snowcapped for most of the winter. In the lowlands the rounded domes of beech and oak, and the towers of elm, match the mood of broad pastures and cornfields in rural landscapes. Beside lakes and rivers the willows, their crowns inclining gracefully towards the broad sunlit water surfaces, appear designed by some master hand to perfect the picture with their contrasts of light and shade.

How Trees are Named

Throughout this book the reader will see that every tree has been given two names. One is its common name in everyday speech, such as 'oak' or 'larch'. The other is its scientific name, which usually requires two words, and sometimes more. This precision is needed because trees grow naturally over large areas, which can include several countries having different languages, so the same tree can have as many names. Beech, for example, is called *hêtre* in French, *Buche* in German, and *faggio* in Italian. These common names are often qualified in various ways, but the status of the difference is rarely clear. American beech, for example, is a distinct botanical species, but copper beech is simply a foliage colour variety of the common European beech.

As the science of botany developed in the seventeenth and eighteenth centuries, botanists felt the need for more exact names that would be understood in all countries. As scholars at that time usually corresponded in Latin, they wisely took the Latin names of the common European trees as their starting point. So oak became *Quercus*, larch became *Larix* and beech became *Fagus*. As explorers travelled farther, and brought back strange plants and trees from countries that the Romans had never known, botanists had to invent fresh names. They were careful always to give them the form of a Latin noun, such as *Eucalyptus* for the Australian gum tree.

This Latin name became the foundation for exact descriptions of the smaller groups of trees. Each of these is called a genus, and the generic title, such as *Fagus,* is usually printed in italics, with a capital letter. All the trees with this scientific name will be found to have similar flowers and fruits. Under the microscope their timbers look much alike, and the nurseryman can graft a scion of one kind of *Fagus* on to a rootstock of another, with every hope of success. Likewise the tree breeder can expect to make hybrids between two trees belonging to the same genus.

The second part of each scientific name, usually printed in italics but with a small initial letter, is the specific name of the kind of tree. *Fagus sylvatica,* or 'beech of the woods' is the European species, while *Fagus grandifolia,* the 'large-leaved beech' is the common American species. This *binomial* system was perfected by the great Swedish naturalist Linnaeus, alias Carl von Linné (1707 to 1778). He named every tree he knew, and appended to its name a concise description in Latin so that any botanist could also, in theory, name any kind after a careful examination.

If finer distinctions are needed, botanists add a third name, for a 'variety' found wild in nature or a 'cultivar' developed under cultivation. The copper beech is *Fagus sylvatica* variety *purpurea.* The finest of several Norway maples is *Acer platanoides* cultivar 'Crimson King'.

In scientific textbooks it is usual to add the name of the 'authority' who first wrote the Latin description of the tree, at the end of this scientific name. Often it is abbreviated, and the letter 'L' is universally accepted for Linnaeus, who established the system. To be valid, the scientific tree name must be supported by an actual specimen of its flowers, fruits, foliage, twigs and bark, called a 'type' specimen. These valuable specimens are carefully preserved in the herbaria, or plant collections, of great national institutions, such as the Royal Botanic Gardens at Kew in Surrey. The Latin description must also be published for anyone to see, usually in a scientific journal of high international repute.

The herbarium can only hold dead specimens. Though it is invariably backed by a great library of books, some illustrated, others just packed with botanical jargon, it remains a lifeless record. The larger botanical centres, therefore, back their herbarium collections with *arboreta,* which are collections of living and growing trees. Thus, the botanical studies of Harvard University are supported by the resources of the great Arnold Arboretum in Boston nearby, and botanists at Kew in London can refer to the gardens at their doorsteps.

The various genera of trees are grouped by botanists in large families of related trees and plants. But this grouping is only of help to advanced students, because our common trees belong either to very small families or else to very large ones! So it is simpler to learn the characteristics of the varied genera themselves, and this book follows that plan.

Though botanists and the nurserymen who grow trees for gardening prefer to use scientific names for trees, the ordinary citizen in every country holds stubbornly to the common names. Inevitably, this preference for well-known names means that some, in every language, get overworked. They are asked to carry the identities of too many trees, all at the same time. So the student must be careful with the 'cedars' (which belong to one genus in America and to others in Asia), the various 'cypresses', and a miscellaneous group of 'pines'. The Englishman's 'plane' becomes the American's 'sycamore', while the American calls the English 'sycamore' – quite correctly – a 'maple'. This brings us back to the original and continuing need for more precise scientific names written in Latin and accepted in all countries.

Above: Winter reveals the full beauty of tree crowns. Here hoar frost outlines, in glistening white, the intricate tracery of birch trees' delicate twigs and graceful branches

The life of a tree: the Oak

An oak tree arises from a seed, the familiar acorn, which is a hard nut that contains two fleshy seed-leaves. Many trees expand their seed-leaves above the ground when they sprout, but the oak keeps them within its hard husk. This splits when, under the warmth of spring, the seed takes in moisture from the damp earth and starts to soften and swell. First it sends down a root that anchors it firmly to the soil. This root bears hairs that explore the crevices in the soil and draw in the constant supply of water that the tree needs for life. This water carries, in solution, minute amounts of mineral salts, particularly those of nitrogen, potassium, phosphorus and iron, which are also essential for growth.

The acorn next sends out an upright shoot, which bears its first green leaves. In the presence of sunlight, water, and the essential mineral salts, these leaves begin the marvellous process called photosynthesis, by which the tree fixes the element carbon (which is always present in the atmosphere in the form of carbon dioxide gas) as carbon compounds. Carbon fixation is carried out by the substance called chlorophyll, which provides the green colour seen in every active leaf.

The resulting compounds provide the main material for building up the tree's substance. They are also its source of the energy needed for growth, because a minute proportion is constantly being consumed, by combination with the oxygen of the air, in a 'breathing' process like that found in the animal world.

The carbon compounds, formed by intricate chemical processes in the leaf, are transported to every part of the seedling, including the roots, as a downward current of sugar sap. Every vein of the oak's leaf is a two-way channel, holding cells that carry root-sap *upwards* ranked close beside others that carry leaf-sap *downwards*. The upward current is always far greater, because a great deal of water is lost from the leaves to the air, in a process called transpiration.

In the woody stems of the oak there are no veins. Instead the downward flow of leaf-sap is

Above right: After pollination, the small bud-like female catkins of oak mature, by autumn, to fruits holding seeds. In pedunculate oak, Quercus robur, *acorns stand on distinct stalks, but the leaves are stalkless*

Right: Short-lived, many flowered male catkins of pedunculate oak open in May, and scatter yellow pollen in the winds

concentrated in the thin outer zone, called bast, just below the protective bark. The actual wood that forms the main bulk of each stem has three functions, namely: support, transport of root-sap upwards towards the leaves and shoots, and the storage of food reserves throughout the winter resting season when the oak stands leafless.

As winter approaches the oak seedling forms a group of winter buds at the tip of its shoot. Its leaves turn brown, fade, and fall away, their stalks breaking off from the woody twig. Growth ceases through the cold season.

The warmth of the following spring causes the oak to put forth fresh leaves to gain more nourishment and substance from the air around it. At the same time its underground roots extend in order to increase its supplies of water and mineral salts. The winter resting buds now burst and certain rapidly dividing cells at the tip of each bud cause the young, tender shoots to elongate.

In this way the tree grows taller and extends its crown. But growth in stem thickness is also essential for its support and active life as it gets bigger. This growth is carried out by a sheath of tissue that surrounds all woody stems, just below their bark. It is called the *cambium* and consists of thin cells that divide rapidly during growing seasons, forming fresh bast cells on its outer surface and fresh wood cells on its inner surface.

In spring, when trees need a lot of sap for their expanding leaves, the cambium forms thin-walled cells with large cavities, called *springwood*. In summer, when strength for support has become more important, it forms thick-walled cells with small cavities, so making *summerwood* which is darker than the springwood. The two zones

are of course circular, and when a woody stem is cut across they can be seen because of the difference in their colour, to make one *annual ring*, representing and recording one year's growth.

The stems of all living trees grow stouter each year. All timber that is actively transporting sap is called *sapwood*. After several years, the inner rings of large stems cease to carry sap, and undergo physical and chemical changes that result in *heartwood*. This is usually darker than the sapwood around it. In many trees, though not in all, it becomes much more durable, particularly when the wood is used as timber exposed to the weather.

Trees, like most other plants, bear flowers. Because they live for long spans of years, they usually postpone flowering and seed-bearing until they are well grown, possibly 30 years old and 50 feet (15·2 m) tall – there are no simple rules here. Once flowering and seed-bearing start, they are continued annually, or every few years, for scores of years thereafter. A single tree may bear hundreds of thousands of seeds.

Some trees, such as cherries, bear flowers which are just like those of common garden plants. There are green sepals to protect them in bud, brightly coloured petals to attract visiting insects, and nectaries to reward these insects with sweet nectar. When a bee arrives it gets dusted with pollen from stamens, and it carries this pollen to the stigma on the pistil of another flower. After receiving pollen, this flower develops a fruit, within the ovary at the base of its pistil, and this fruit includes the seed that can later sprout to become another tree.

The oak, however, bears its flowers as catkins, which are clusters of simpler flowers. Its pollen is carried by the wind, so there are no petals, no

perfume and no nectar. Each catkin is either male or female, though both grow on the same tree. Male catkins, which open in April and last for only a few weeks before withering, form groups of long stalks bearing numerous small flowers. Each flower consists of green protective bracts and yellow stamens, with anthers that scatter pollen on the wind.

The female catkins, which open at the same time, form clusters of two or three bud-like structures, built up of green bracts, with a central pistil. After the stigma at the tip of this pistil has caught wind-borne pollen, a fertilized female ovule at the pistil's base develops rapidly to become a ripe seed – the nut we call the acorn. Bracts at its base fuse together, become woody, and develop into the brown acorn cup that supports the nut. In the following autumn the brown acorn falls from its cup onto the forest floor, and the life cycle of another oak tree begins.

In theory, a big tree like an oak has the power to live for an indefinite span of years, getting bigger all the time. In practice there are limits to its age and size. Few oaks live for more than 500 years, grow taller than 120 feet (36·6 m), or reach a girth, measured at the conventional point, called breast height, about $4\frac{1}{4}$ feet (1·3 m) above the ground, of more than 40 feet (12·2 m).

Young oaks face many dangers, including insects, fungal diseases, damage by animals and birds, and harm done by abnormal weather, including fierce gales or severe drought. Most of them, however, perish through being crowded out by other trees, including their own brother oaks. Older, established trees have fewer serious enemies, but if they are not deliberately felled for timber, they eventually fall victim to internal decay. Branches break away in high winds, and the wounds they leave offer points of entry to the spores of wood-rotting fungi. Although it becomes very durable when felled, the heartwood of a living oak is slowly broken down by the fine threads of the fungus until the sapwood, branches and foliage around it lack sufficient support. Then, one windy day, the great tree crashes to the ground and its life is ended.

Above: At Arbroath on the east coast of Scotland, oak is still used for the keel and ribs of fishing boats. The planking is European larch

The Oaks

Oaks of various kinds are dominant trees in many European, American and Asiatic forests. The main species in western Europe is the **pedunculate oak,** *Quercus robur.* This tree has also been widely planted as a shade tree in the eastern United States, and even in South Africa, New Zealand and Australia. True oaks can be identified at any time of the year by a key feature that characterizes them all. The buds and leaves, though set singly along the twigs, are clustered close to the twig tips. Because the shoots develop from the buds, this pattern is reflected in the oak's rugged, irregular pattern of branching. The pedunculate oak is distinguished by the long stalks on its female flowers and on the acorns that follow. Its leaves, by contrast, have no stalk and bear distinctive lobes, called auricles, at their base.

Another species common in Europe's deciduous oakwoods, and very similar to the pedunculate oak, is the **sessile oak,** *Q. petraea,* which, as its name suggests, bears sessile or stalkless female flowers and acorns directly on the woody twigs. Its leaves however have long stalks but no auricles at their base. Pure woods of only one of these species of oak are rare. Hybrid trees, with intermediate characteristics, are common.

Both these common European oaks have leaves with a characteristic wavy outline, technically called pinnately lobed. Both have clustered buds with many brown scales. The bark is smooth and brownish-grey on young trees. It becomes very thick and rough on old trunks, and breaks up into a characteristic pattern of irregular squares. The sessile oak keeps a distinct leading shoot longer, forming the straighter timber stem, but both kinds eventually develop spreading crowns with countless twisted branches. Their trunks attain great girths. Records for British trees are 120 feet (36·6 m) tall and 43 feet (13·1 m) round for pedunculate oak, and 135 feet (41·1 m) tall and 30 feet (9·1 m) round for sessile oak.

Many of the stoutest oaks are 'pollard' trees, which were lopped in days gone by to provide firewood from their branches. This was done about six feet (1·8 m) up, so that the young shoots that sprang from the lopped trunk started growth safely above the reach of browsing cattle. Pollards can be recognized because their short trunks are topped by stout, spreading branches.

In nature, both these oaks hold their own well in competition with other trees. Their large seeds, which are spread accidentally by seed-eating birds like jays or pigeons, and seed-eating animals like squirrels, give the seedlings a good start. Once established, their long life span proves an advantage for the survival of the species.

Oaks are easily raised from acorns in forest nurseries provided they are carefully stored through the winter under naturally moist conditions. The seedlings thrive when transplanted

Right: The sturdy trunk and deeply ridged, furrowed bark of a giant pedunculate oak. Note the buttressed base and the round patterns where scars left by fallen branches have healed

to the forest. Oak is still regularly planted, even though it takes at least a century to mature. The forester's long-term reward is a particularly valuable and beautiful timber.

Oak logs have a thin, yellow, outer sapwood zone which, though strong, has no natural durability and soon perishes if used untreated out of doors. Within lies the rich brown heartwood – the famous 'heart of oak' which is very strong, hard, naturally durable, yet easily worked with the right tools and techniques. It has been valued since the earliest times for building houses, barns, churches, and wooden ships of all kinds. It is also the best timber for fencing, including gate posts, the gates themselves, lesser upright posts and rails. Indoors it makes attractive, strong, durable joinery and furniture, particularly tables, benches, dressers, and chests, which often show beautifully figured grain. Specialized uses include

ladder rungs, spokes for wooden wheels, and staves for beer barrels and sherry casks since this wood can, when cut in the right way, safely retain alcoholic spirits as well as water. In the past, oak charcoal was used in the process of making iron and as an ingredient in gunpowder. An excellent commercial tannin, for tanning hides into leather, was extracted from oak bark on a large scale.

Turkey oak, *Q. cerris,* which comes from Asia Minor and is occasionally planted as a vigorous ornamental tree, is distinguished from the European oaks by its longer leaf, with more zig-zag, sawtooth pattern edges. At the base of each leaf stalk it bears conspicuous slender bracts (leaf-like scales), called stipules. Its acorn cups are clad in soft leafy bracts too, hence the name moss-cupped oak. Fissures in its grey bark show an orange shade. Its timber is highly esteemed in

Above: Pollard oak in summer. Pollarding, now rarely done, is the lopping of trunks at head height to secure repeated crops of small poles and firewood

Turkey, but faster growth in western Europe results in an unreliable material, apt to warp and shrink unduly. The tree which is known in America as Turkey oak, is actually a distinct native species, *Q. laevis*. It has a similar leaf shape and thrives on sandy soils in Florida.

Evergreen oak, *Q. ilex,* also called the holm oak from its resemblance to a holly tree, is an evergreen species native to the Mediterranean. Its evergreen habit is an adaptation to the Mediterranean climate of hot, dry summers and warm, moist winters. The leaves remain active all the year round, but they can resist drought. They are oval in shape, tough, and glossy, a very dark green above and pale green below. When new leaves open in May, they are soft and pale green, and clad in whitish down. They last for about three years, then turn dull brown and fall. Evergreen oak's dense crown casts a deep shade, and its black bark is broken into countless small irregular squares. The male catkins are yellowish-white. The small, green, female flowers develop into fruits consisting of hard, rounded acorns set in shallow cups. The timber is very hard and dense, dark brown in colour, with rose-pink mottling. Though difficult to work, it is used in France and Italy for furniture and ornamental work. Its dense substance makes ideal firewood.

Above: Sessile oak, Quercus petraea, *bears stalkless acorns, but its leaves have distinct stalks*

Right: Turkey or moss-cupped oak, Quercus cerris, *bears acorns in cups clad with shaggy bracts. Its long leaves have saw-tooth outlines*

11

North America has a remarkable range of native oaks, numbering 40 in all. The most valuable commercially are the **white oaks,** such as *Q. alba,* found mainly in the eastern states, but with representatives in California and Oregon also. Most of these have lobed leaves very similar to those of the common European oaks. A few, such as the chestnut oak, *Q. prinus,* bear leaves with sawtooth edges, like those of the sweet chestnut of the genus *Castanea.* The white oaks yield timbers comparable in every way to the best European material and with similar uses.

The south-eastern states, and the Californian region, have several native evergreen oaks, known as **live oaks,** which resemble the Mediterranean species and are adapted to similar climates. Typical species are the common live oak, *Q. virginiana,* native to the south-east and the California live oak, *Q. agrifolia.*

Red oaks, the commonest group throughout the eastern United States, are distinguished by the crimson or scarlet colour that runs through their dark green foliage and leaf stalks. It is apparently a device to lessen the drying effect of hot summer sunshine. In autumn this colour takes on an amazing brillance, rivalling that of the maple. Red oaks have a typical flame-shaped leaf outline, running out into angular, pointed lobes. Their acorns take 18 months to ripen, instead of the usual six. Red oak timber lacks the strength and durability of white or European oak, but proves a good general-purpose material.

The striking autumn colours of the red oaks have led to their widespread planting in England, Italy and other European countries, as unusual ornamental trees. The hardiest and most commonly grown kinds are the northern red oak, *Q. rubra,* and the scarlet oak, *Q. coccinea.*

Above left: a sapling North American red oak, Quercus borealis, *flaming with bright colour before its leaves fall in autumn*

Above: Evergreen oak, Quercus ilex, *seen here in winter, makes an impressive, tall tree with dark green, tough leaves like those of laurel*

Beeches and Sweet Chestnut

The **beech** can be recognized at once, whatever its size and age, by the smooth, metallic grey bark that clothes its trunk and branches. In looking at a fruiting twig you may observe the typical oval leaf, spiny green seed husk, and the smooth, brown, triangular nut. Beech foliage checks the passage of light more effectively than most other tree crowns can do, and, on the deeply shaded floor of a beechwood no small green plants can thrive. You walk on a carpet of last year's faded tan-brown leaves, which will ultimately break down to make a rich leaf mould.

All beech trees belong to the genus *Fagus* in the Fagaceae or beech family. The European species is *Fagus sylvatica,* and the American one, which resembles it very closely but has larger leaves, is *F. grandifolia.* A remarkable and beautiful variety is the copper beech, first discovered in Germany in the eighteenth century, and, since then, propagated by grafting. In this form the natural green of the foliage is masked by deep copper-brown or purplish pigments, and a large specimen makes a strong contrast with all the neighbouring trees with their normal green hues. Beech is often grown as a hedge bush, for it stands clipping well. Remarkably, it holds its faded, dead, fawny brown leaves right through winter, providing extra shelter and ornament.

The natural spread of beechwoods is limited by their need for warm summers to ripen their heavy crops of seed. They are found throughout the hill ranges of central and southern Europe, and also in eastern America, but usually on the foothills rather than the upper ridges. At higher levels the beeches give way to spruces or silver firs, which need less warmth. On the plains most beechwoods were cleared long ago for cultivation on the deep soils enriched by the leaf mould.

In Britain, beech is not native north of the Midlands, though it has been widely planted in Scotland. It is Denmark's national tree, but its homeland only reaches to the south of Sweden and to the southernmost tip of Norway.

Beech tolerates calcium better than most trees, and the finest stands, or groups, often grow on chalk or limestone soils. In the past, many old beeches were lopped or pollarded. The regrowth of branches provided firewood.

The seasonal life of the beech begins in April, when the long, brown, pointed buds burst to reveal bright, pale green leaves. These will darken later, and finally turn orange-brown

Right: In May, male flowers of beech open in yellow tassels on long-stalked hanging catkins, amid emerald green leaves. Smaller female catkins stand upright and resemble buds

Following pages: Morning mist catches an aura of golden sunlight surrounding the russet foliage and shapely trunk of this fine beech

before falling in October. Spring also sees the opening of short-lived male catkins, little tassels of stamens on long stalks, which scatter golden pollen. The bud-like female catkins ripen after pollination to become autumn fruits, in the form of green spiny husks holding brown nuts. Squirrels, pigeons, and many other beasts and birds devour these, but enough escape to provide seedlings for future beechwoods.

Beech timber is an even, pale brown colour, shot through with red-brown specks. Being strong, hard and capable of being shaped to a smooth finish in any direction, it is very valuable commercially. Most is used for furniture, or for short tool handles and wooden utensils such as bowls, spoons, mallet heads, or blocks for carpenters' planes.

Sweet chestnut, *Castanea sativa,* is Italy's gift to the forests of northern Europe. In the days of the Roman Empire, colonizing generals carried its nuts across the Alps into Germany, where it is nowadays called *Kastanie,* to France where it became *châtaignier* and its fruit *marron,* and to England where Anglo-Saxons later called it chestnut. These names for the tree all come from the same Latin source. The reason for chestnut's spread was of course its nutritious and delicious nut. The nuts were ground into a flour which, as polenta, formed a staple food for marching legionaries. You can also roast the nuts, boil them for turkey stuffing, or crystallize them with sugar to make *marrons glacés.* The tree is also called 'Spanish chestnut', because of the large Spanish export trade in the nuts.

The huge, pointed, oval leaf of the sweet chestnut marks it out at once. Set singly on the stout stem, it is often as much as ten inches (250 mm) long. It is short-stalked and it has

distinctive 'teeth' on its edge like saw teeth. In summer, this leaf is dark green above and paler below. It fades to yellowish-gold in autumn. In winter, sweet chestnut can be identified by its sturdy twigs, its large purplish-brown buds, and its bold bark pattern. Large stems carry a network of grey-brown ribs, often twisted spirally.

Sweet chestnuts flower in July, opening groups of bright yellow catkins that contrast with the dark green foliage. Each catkin has a long central stalk that bears clusters of male flowers, each being a group of numerous stamens shedding golden pollen. Near the base of the catkin a few small, bud-shaped female flowers develop. Some of these become pollinated by the wind but the flowers of both sexes bear nectaries, and much pollen is carried from flower to flower by nectar-seeking bees. By October, the female flowers ripen to the well-known chestnuts, bright

brown, triangular-oval nuts which are enclosed, often in pairs, within a tough, green, spiny husk. Those few nuts that escape being gathered by people, or being eaten on the spot by hungry mice, squirrels, pheasants or pigeons, sprout the next spring. Each sends up a sturdy shoot bearing typical oval leaves. Chestnuts have become naturalized in many countries to which they have been introduced, but the seed cannot ripen in the colder, northern countries.

Chestnut timber is remarkable for the thickness of its golden-brown, strong and durable heartwood. This is surrounded by a narrow zone of yellow, perishable sapwood, only about $\frac{1}{2}$ inch (13 mm) thick. This peculiarity makes it particularly valuable for fencing and similar work in contact with damp ground, since heartwood resists decay for 50 years or more. Chestnut is widely used for fence posts. In the English county of Kent it serves as sturdy supports for the wires and strings used to carry the climbing hop plants which yield an essential ingredient of bitter beer.

If you cut back a chestnut tree, a thicket of sturdy stems shoots up from its stump. These stems are widely used for fencing and firewood. In Kent they are cleft by hand into tough pales (long, thin, wedge-shaped pieces of timber) which are then woven on to wires to make serviceable 'cleft pale' fencing. Unfortunately, bigger timber is apt to split, so chestnut is rarely used for fine joinery or furniture.

Chestnut wood and bark are rich in tannin. In Italy a tannin extract for turning hides into leather is obtained by boiling branchwood and cheft timber. After slicing into strips, this material can be cunningly woven, by hand, into strong yet light baskets.

The native American chestnut, *Castanea dentata*, was formerly a leading forest tree throughout the eastern United States, and a valued source of timber, firewood, fencing and tannins. Alas, tragedy struck in the 1930s, when the chestnut blight fungus, *Endothia parasitica*, was accidentally brought in on Chinese chestnut trees destined for a botanical garden. The American chestnut proved highly susceptible to this fungus, and whole forests perished. Perhaps one day these forests may be rebuilt by using disease-resistant strains.

Chestnuts can reach great size—often exceeding 100 feet (30·5 m) in height. A tree at Tortworth in Gloucestershire, England, possibly a group of stems from a stump cut hundreds of years ago, is 52 feet (15·8 m) round. Another, at Canford in Dorset, is probably Britain's stoutest single tree, with a girth of 43 feet (13·1 m).

17

Birch and Alder

The shining white bark of **birch** trees marks them out at once in mountain or northern landscapes. This unique colour is not seen on young twigs but develops, as each trunk becomes thicker, through a special layer of cells which produces the gleaming white covering. The advantage of white, as against a darker shade, is that it loses less heat by radiation, yet, through reflection, gives a greater resistance to scorching by hot sunshine. This temperature control, though only a matter of a few critical degrees, helps birch to thrive farther north, and higher up the mountains, than any other broadleaved tree.

Birch bark is tough, and waterproof too. It strips off the tree naturally, but the North American Indians found that they could remove it in large sheets and use it as the covering for canoes. The canoes were strong enough to carry men and stores, yet light enough to be carried from one river system to another. This device, quickly adopted by early French Canadian explorers, opened up vast areas of the North American continent. Alpine dwellers use birch bark to make alphorns, those quaint, huge yet light musical instruments that can send a tune far across a mountain valley. The Lapps of the tundra use the bark for baskets, belts, plates, or waterproof roofing for their huts.

Birch bears exceptionally thin, strong, purplish-brown twigs, which are widely used for sweeping brooms, and at one time were used by teachers to chastise, or 'birch', wayward schoolboys. Foresters also use them as fire-beaters.

The very small buds, set singly along these twigs, burst in April to release small, short-stalked leaves, which are oval, triangular or diamond-shaped, and have toothed edges. Pale green at first, they darken later.

Just before the leaves open in spring, the male catkins, which have been visible as curved brown structures, rather like caterpillars, expand and turn green. Their clusters of bracts open to expose minute petals and golden stamens which scatter yellow pollen on the wind. This is caught by female catkins, which have by now expanded from tiny buds to become oblong structures, also shaped like caterpillars, but smaller than the males. Each female catkin holds many groups of tiny flowers set among green bracts. Each individual flower has two protruding stigmas, which look like bristles along the 'caterpillar', and a basal ovary.

Below left: In September, birch's plump, mature female fruiting catkins turn brown and shatter, releasing winged seeds

Below: In April, male catkins of birch droop in 'lamb's tail' shapes from slender twigs, amid newly opened leaves. Green female catkins are much smaller and curve upwards

Above: Silver birches displaying their white-barked trunks and graceful crowns of delicate foliage

Following pages: Leafless alders beside a frozen pond

half-round wooden objects, like the heads of sweeping brooms, are made from birch timber in country workshops. The usual method involves turning, that is spinning the wood against a fixed metal chisel.

In Scandinavia and Canada birch is widely used for everyday furniture. Large logs are peeled by powerful machines to yield sheets of timber called veneers. These are made up, with interleaved veneers of spruce, into birch-faced plywood, to give an attractive, creamy-brown surface that is both smooth and hard wearing.

Birch makes a first-rate firewood. Stacks of logs are a familiar sight around farmsteads in Alpine and northern regions. Unfailingly, birchwoods renew the supply, essential to life in the upland hills. They also give shelter to sheep and cattle against winter snowstorms.

Birches are the typical trees of the birch family, or Betulaceae. The commonest species in most of Europe is the silver birch, *Betula pendula*, which is distinguished by smooth twigs that bear little swellings or warts. The hairy birch, *B. pubescens*, which tends to grow on more marshy soils and farther north than the silver birch, can be recognized by its downy twigs, which lack swellings. Dwarf birch, *B. nana*, is a bushy form with rounded teeth on its leaf edges which thrives on high mountains and in northern Russia and Scandinavia. The principal American species is the paper birch, *B. papyrifera*, which is found right across Canada and the northern United States, and has much larger leaves than the European kinds. In Alaska the shrubby ground birch, *B. rotundifolia*, is important as a food for reindeer.

Alders are found along watersides, or in swamps, because their little seedlings only grow effectively in damp mud near the waterline. Although they are broadleaved trees, and lose their leaves in winter, they are easily recognized all the year round by their 'cones', odd woody structures very similar, in appearance and function, to those borne by true coniferous trees like pines and spruces.

In winter the alders can also be identified by their club-shaped buds. These purplish-brown structures are set singly along the dull-brown twigs, and have a narrow base and a swollen tip. The future male catkins are also evident at this time as sausage-shaped, grey-brown structures grouped in twos or threes. In March, before the leaves open, the male catkins enlarge and hang down like lambs' tails. Their numerous separate flowers, each a group of bracts and stamens, scatter yellow, wind-borne pollen. Meanwhile the female catkins, borne in clusters, have

During the summer the fertilized female catkins expand to become much larger, greenish-brown cylinders, which, in September, suddenly ripen and shatter, releasing winged seeds and spent bracts.

Birch seeds, each a minute grain surrounded by a papery, brown wing, are wafted by the million over forest and mountainside. Scarcely one seedling in a thousand survives to sprout on a patch of bare soil or in some cranny of the rocks, yet foresters always find enough birch trees without planting any.

Birch timber is a uniform pale brown colour, with a dull surface. There is no apparent distinction between heartwood and sapwood, and birch is regarded as 'perishable', because it lasts only a few years if employed outside. If kept dry, however, it proves strong, tough, and durable. Tool handles, bobbins, and other small round or

expanded from small buds to green globes, each made up of many bracts and pistils. After pollination, they enlarge rapidly into soft, green spherical cones which measure about $\frac{1}{4}$ inch (6 mm) across.

By autumn these cones have become hard, woody, and dark brown. The former soft bracts, now tough scales, open to release the seeds. They then persist on the trees as spent cones for a year or so.

Each little alder seed has a pair of floats that help to keep it airborne on a strong wind, or else to float down a river or across a lake until it has been stranded on some muddy shore. There it sprouts, sending up two oval seed-leaves, followed by curious, lobed and pointed early leaves, and eventually by normal foliage. Alders only grow vigorously in soil that holds a remarkable organism called *Schinzia alni*. This forms nodules on the alder's roots, and enables the tree to 'fix' the free nitrogen of the air. This aids the alder's nutrition, and as time goes by, the swamps in which alders grow gradually become fertile through the break-down of fallen nitrogen-rich leaves and branches.

Alder timber is pinkish-brown and relatively soft, with no great merits of strength or durability. It is easily carved, however, and it resists water.

Above: Alders in rich green summer foliage beside a river, a typical waterside habitat

These properties ensure its use in wooden footwear, including the sabots and clogs once widely worn in north-western England. It is also used, like birch, for broom-heads, tool handles, toys and other small, cheap, wooden articles. When freshly felled, the cut surface shows a brilliant orange colour, but this colour fades after several days.

Red dyes can be obtained from alder bark, green from the catkins, and yellow from young shoots. The bark can also be used for tanning leather.

Huge alder swamps—known in northern and eastern England as 'carrs' from their Norse name of *kjarr*—once covered the lowland river valleys of northern Europe. But farmers everywhere slowly cleared and drained them in order to use their fertile, fen-peat soils.

The common alder, *Alnus glutinosa*, is known by deep-green round leaves, with toothed edges, which fade to dark grey before they fall. Grey alder, *A. incana*, has pale green oval leaves, and the Italian alder, *A. cordata*, has mid-green heart-shaped ones. The commonest American species is the shrubby, speckled alder, *A. rugosa*, of the eastern United States. On the west coast the red alder, *A. rubra*, grows vigorously to timber size.

Left: In March, before their leaves expand, alders open long, drooping male catkins. Much smaller, knob-shaped female catkins, shown top and left in this picture, develop later into woody 'cones' like the one in the centre

Hornbeam and Hazel

Hornbeams grow in the south of England, across Europe and in the temperate regions of North America, but they are not hardy in northern areas. Most people mistake them at first for beech trees, because they have similar bark and leaves, but the bole, or trunk, of a hornbeam is irregular in outline, and bears a network of silvery, shining ribs over its mainly steel-grey surface. The leaves have strongly marked parallel veins, and a distinctly toothed edge, not seen on beech. The winter buds, set singly, are shorter than those of beech and are always bent inwards towards the twigs. Hornbeam never becomes a very large tree, its greatest height being 85 feet (25·9 m) and its biggest girth only 13 feet (4 m).

Hornbeam flowers develop as separate male and female catkins, which open in April on the same tree. Male catkins bear many clusters of small, green male flowers, each of which is a cluster of stamens ready to shed yellow pollen in the springtime winds. The female catkins, also green, are smaller, more erect and leafy. Each blade is a green bract bearing two flowers with two styles apiece, and six bracteoles. During summer the bracteoles expand to form remarkable, papery, three-lobed wings, peculiar to hornbeam. They change from green to pale brown, as the hanging branches of fruits ripen in autumn, and their purpose is to carry the seeds through the air. The seed, or nutlet, matures at the base of each wing. It is a small, brown, oval object with a ribbed skin. Birds, mice and

Right: Hornbeam can be recognized by its irregular, fluted trunk, which shows a network of bright, metallic-grey ridges

squirrels take many of these nutritious morsels, but those that escape destruction sprout 18 months after ripening. The seedling first bears two seed-leaves, which are oval with concave bases, and then normal foliage.

Hornbeam draws its name from the exceptionally hard and horny character of its wood. This is an even, creamy-brown in colour, and has low natural durability out of doors. Indoors it will serve for years as a hard bench top, standing the toughest wear. Butchers' chopping blocks are always made of hornbeam, set with its grain upright to resist constant cutting with sharp knives. In the past hornbeam provided durable cogs for machinery, especially in windmills and watermills, before metals were adopted. It was

also used for ox-yokes, when oxen drew ploughs and carts, because it was tough and wore smoothly. It is still used for the hammer mechanisms in pianos.

Hornbeam makes a first rate firewood and its twigs are good kindling. Epping Forest near London holds thousands of pollard hornbeams, once lopped by countrymen for fuelwood and faggots. In nearby Kent there are many shrubby coppices, which were once cut back, every ten years or so, for the same purpose. In gardens hornbeams are often planted for hedges. They stand clipping well, making a close screen, and they hold their faded, fawny-brown leaves all through the winter.

The common European hornbeam is *Carpinus betulus*. The American hornbeam, *C. caroliniana*, often called the water beech, thrives in swampy woods all through the eastern United States.

Hazel, though never a large tree, has played a leading part in country life in Western Europe since prehistoric times. Its slender, smooth-barked, grey-brown stems are tough yet supple. If you cut them back to the stump, a fresh crop will spring up, which you can harvest about seven years later. This practice, called coppicing, produced the hazel 'copses' of England and many other European countries. It ensures a steady supply of wooden rods which have a remarkable range of uses. Hazel rods may become firewood, kindling, beansticks, supports for vines or tomatoes, spars or 'brooches' for holding thatch on cottage roofs or cornstacks, or they can become handy walking sticks.

Hurdles are a form of light, cheap, portable fence made by hand from hazel rods. The hurdle-maker, a skilled craftsman, sets up a frame of stout round rods, and then, using a billhook, cleaves thinner stems into pliant strips. He inter-weaves these strips into his frame, twisting and binding them so that the hurdle holds together without any other fasteners. Similar hurdles, known as 'wattles', were used all over Europe to make walls for farm buildings, cottages, and even substantial houses. They were set in frames of oak, being bent or 'sprung' so that their ends engaged in slots and could not later fall out. They were then daubed with stiff wet clay, to make a 'wattle-and-daub' wall which, if kept dry, could endure for centuries.

Early in February the hazel provides one of the gayest woodland sights by displaying, on its bare leafless branches, the hanging 'lambs' tails' that are its male catkins. These expand from the grey-brown oval buds in which they have passed the winter, and reveal their numerous flowers, each a group of yellow stamens below a green

Left: Hornbeam foliage and fruits in September. Each three-lobed green wing bears a tiny nut at its base

Right: Hard-shelled, but delicious, hazel nuts ripen in leafy husks in October amid round, deeply veined leaves

Left: In February, hazel opens golden male catkins, hanging from leafless twigs. The bud-shaped female catkins are much smaller and are tipped with crimson stigmas

Right: Sunlight strikes through a hazel coppice. Bushes like these are cut back at intervals to provide pea sticks, bean rods, and material for making hurdles

bract. Their abundant pollen is wafted by spring breezes through the woods, unhindered by any foliage. At this stage few people notice the much smaller female catkins, for each looks like a small green bud. Their identity is revealed by the tuft of crimson stigmas, which catch the drifting pollen.

In April the leaves expand from their oval green buds, set singly along the grey-brown, sinuous twigs. They are oval to heart-shaped in outline, with short stalks, toothed edges, and a bluntly pointed tip. They are a restful mid-green colour, and fade in autumn to a golden-yellow shade.

As summer advances each female catkin expands rapidly to become a cluster of nuts, each surrounded by a cup of large leafy bracts derived from the small green bracts of the flower. Each nut is the fruit of a single one-seeded flower. It has a hard, woody shell holding a delicious and nutritious kernel, which has a soft brown skin around firm white flesh. Hazel nuts, also called cobs, or, in some varieties, filberts, are widely eaten alone or else made up into confectionery or nut chocolate. The main supplies come from the Mediterranean lands or from Iran, where good nut crops ripen under hot sunshine, though a few nut orchards are tended in the southern English county of Kent, and there are others in America.

Nut gatherers, which include squirrels, field mice, jays, pigeons, pheasants, and children, flock to the hazel copses in October. But a few of the nuts escape destruction and sprout next spring to fill gaps in the crop of bushes. The seed-leaves remain as storage organs in the nut at ground level, and the shoot that arises bears bracts first, followed by normal foliage.

Throughout England and much of western Europe it has long been customary to grow hazel as 'underwood', below taller, so-called standard trees, usually oak or ash. These standards yielded, at long intervals, the big timbers needed for building houses, barns, bridges, ships or farm waggons, while the more plentiful hazel was cut every seven years to yield the smaller pieces needed in greater quantities. Hazel coppices make good cover for pheasants and indeed for wild animals and birds of every kind, and they are remarkably rich in spring flowers. Many are now maintained as nature reserves.

America has three native hazels. American hazel, *Corylus americana*, is found in the eastern States, along with the beaked hazel, *C. rostrata*, which has its fruit bracts prolonged into a narrow snout. California hazel, *C. cornuta* var. *californica*, is a tall shrub with similarly beaked fruit which grows in the west.

Poplars and Willows

Poplars form a remarkable group of broadleaved trees, distinguished above all by their long-stalked leaves, which flutter in the slightest breeze. The French Canadian folk name for aspen poplar, *langues de femme*, or women's tongues, obviously derives from their unceasing motion!

Because of their constant movement, poplar leaves transpire water rapidly, just as a wet cloth waved in the wind dries quickly. So foresters rank them as 'thirsty' trees that only flourish in marshes or along riversides. They reach their finest development and scenic grandeur when planted in stately avenues along the canals and rivers of France or northern Italy. Their greed for water is reflected in the peculiar character of their timber, which is yellowish-white, soft, and composed mainly of large water-carrying vessels. When it is full of sap, as in the growing tree, the wood is heavy, but after felling and seasoning it becomes exceptionally light, and, incidentally, a poor firewood. In America both timber and tree are aptly called 'cottonwood'.

Though only moderately strong, poplar timber is exceptionally supple, and most of it is used in special ways. Trees are specially grown at wide spacings of around 30 feet (9·1 m) and branches are pruned from their lower stems so that these stems hold no knots. After felling, the resulting logs are 'turned' in a huge lathe that peels off long sheets of thin white veneer. One important use for this is to make the light, strong baskets in which fruit and vegetables are packed for transport in France, Spain and Italy. Smaller strips are used for match boxes. All wooden matches are made from similar poplar veneers, cut somewhat thicker, then sliced by automatic machines into millions of little stalks, which are later dipped into the chemical that forms their striking heads. Only poplar is tough enough to stand the strain of striking a stick of such a small dimension, and porous enough to hold the paraffin wax that burns with a clear flame. Further, its smouldering ash holds together, not falling and creating a fire risk as the ash of other timbers would do.

Left: Plantation of hybrid black poplars. Spaced far apart, these saplings show slender, erect stems and heart-shaped leaves, that tremble in the slightest breeze

Other uses of this versatile wood are as paper pulp, joinery planks, light packing cases, and in high-grade chipboard. Not surprisingly, poplars are widely planted by farmers throughout fertile, well-drained yet well-watered marshlands in Italy, France, the Netherlands and England. They grow remarkably fast, often maturing at only 30 years, with stems 90 feet (27·4 m) tall and 6 feet (1·8 m) round. The record for height in England is 140 feet (42·7 m), and that for girth, 21 feet (6·4 m), both held by a Black Italian poplar at Tonbridge in Kent. A pleasing feature of poplar plantations is their light shade, so that in their early years farm crops can be cultivated between the trees. Later, grasses growing among the poplars provide lush grazing for cattle.

The characteristics of poplar bark vary with the species, from a smooth and shining pale grey in the white poplar, to a thick, grey, rugged

Right: Fading leaves of aspen poplars aflame with bright golden colours in the autumn sun

Far right: Black Italian poplar, a hybrid between European and American species, grows vigorously in lowland hedgerows. The uneven-sided, open crown seen here is characteristic

Right: Male catkins of grey poplar open on leafless twigs in March. One drooping catkin holds many flowers, each a group of yellow stamens below a pink bract

armour, broken into squares, in the so-called 'black' hybrids. Twigs are usually sturdy, with ridges ending in prominent leaf scars below oval, stout buds, which are grouped or set singly and show several scales. Buds are often waxy, and in balsam poplars the wax becomes pleasantly fragrant in spring. Many poplars show bold, asymmetric branching, and many look more like a huge branch stuck in the ground than a well-balanced tree. A key feature for identifying poplars is the random branching of the veins in their leaves—never the same on both sides of the mid-rib. The leaves can be round, heart-shaped, triangular, or sometimes lobed.

Every poplar is either male or female. If cuttings are taken they keep the sex of their parent tree. Female trees are rare in gardens, because their fluffy seeds litter tidy paths or stick to wet paint. Both sexes flower in March, before the

Left: Lombardy poplars, shown here where they first arose on the North Italian plain, display beautiful, slender outlines. All their small side branches follow the main trunk upwards

Right: Stirred by spring winds, this tall white poplar in an English hedgerow reveals the lovely silver undersides of its green leaves

leaves open, and pollen is carried by the wind. Male flowers open in long, loose-hanging catkins that look like fat caterpillars, with blossoms in small groups along the main stalk. Each flower has one green bract and many crimson stamens that shed golden pollen. Female flowers also open in clusters on a hanging stalk; their catkin as a whole looks like a string of beads. Each female flower consists of one green bract beside a green pistil. After pollination this pistil expands, to become, by mid-summer, a small tough-skinned green pod. It then splits, and releases scores of tiny black seeds, each bearing a tuft of white hairs that aids the seed's travels in the wind.

Poplar seeds only germinate successfully if they land on damp mud, usually in marshes or beside rivers, within a few days. Each seed produces two oval, green seed-leaves, followed by typical 'adult' foliage. Under cultivation most poplars are increased by cuttings which, in most varieties, take root readily. Tree breeders have raised many desirable hybrids from seed, each with such merits as fast growth or good form.

The hardiest poplars are **European aspen,** *Populus tremula* and its close ally **American aspen,** *P. tremuloides*. Both grow beside creeks in the tundra, or far up high mountains, on soil frozen for much of the year. They form thickets that spread by root suckers (new plants springing up from the roots) or by seeding, but they will not normally strike root from cuttings. Aspens can be recognized through their incessantly quivering round leaves (the French call these trees *trembles*), which hang from thin flattened stalks and have bluntly toothed margins. The autumn colour of the leaves is a brilliant gold. Aspen wood makes the best matches.

Farther south in Europe thrive the lovely

white poplar, *P. alba* and the allied **grey poplar,** *P. canescens.* Key characteristics of these trees are pale bark, lobed leaves on vigorous shoots, and a shining white underside, clad in felt-like hairs, to the otherwise dark green leaf. This makes a marvellous colour contrast when the spring winds stir their tall crowns.

Black poplars, so-called by contrast, have grey bark and mid-green foliage. The common European kind is *P. nigra*, while the most widespread eastern American species is *P. deltoides*. The best known hybrid between them, which probably originated in Italy, is the Black Italian poplar, *P.* 'Serotina'. Its varietal name signifies 'late leafing'. Although its bronze-coloured leaf buds do not break until late April or early May it grows rapidly during its short season.

Lombardy poplar, so-called from its abundance on the plains of the Po Valley in northern Italy, is an exceptional variety, *italica*, of European black poplar. All its side branches follow the upward trend of the main trunk, giving a graceful outline like a tall flame or plume of feathers. The frequent knots make its stem useless for timber, but it is valued for tall, narrow screens to check winds or hide buildings. Few other trees can rival it for scenic effect.

Balsam poplars, native to North America but often planted in Europe, owe their name to the sticky coating of their buds, which sends a powerful fragrance through the woods in spring. They bear oval, pointed, mid-green leaves and have black bark. The common balsam poplar, *P. balsamifera*, thrives across Canada and the northern United States. Black cottonwood or giant balsam, *P. trichocarpa*, found only in the west, reaches 225 feet (68·6 m) in Oregon river valleys and is the tallest recorded poplar, with girths up to 25 feet (7·6 m).

The word **willow** immediately suggests a tree with branches drooping gracefully over a river or still lake. Many willows do in fact grow in this way, though their weeping habit is not caused by sadness, but by the practical attraction of sunlight, reflected from the water surface. They enjoy direct sunlight from above, too, and this double illumination may explain why they are always the first trees to break into bright green leaf in March, and the last trees to lose their withered, grey-brown foliage in November.

Poetic associations of willows with sadness are found almost universally, for instance in the Chinese story celebrated in the willow-pattern. In Shakespeare's *Hamlet*, when Gertrude tells of the death of Ophelia, she says: 'There is a willow grows aslant a brook.' In the Bible this tree became linked to the Israelites' exile: 'By the rivers of Babylon, there we sat down, yea we wept, when we remembered Zion. We hanged our harps upon the willows in the midst thereof.' (Ps. 137:1-2.)

The commonest cultivated weeping willow is the variety *tristis*—literally 'the sad one'—of the European white willow, *Salix alba*. An Asiatic species, *S. babylonica*, grows in China and also in Iraq, where, in 1730, it was found thriving beside the Euphrates by an English merchant named Vernon.

Weeping strains are also found among American, Australian, and South African willows. The fact that these singular trees have a world-wide spread proves a very ancient origin.

A key feature of all willows, aiding identification, is the presence of only one visible exterior scale enclosing each oval winter bud. These buds are set singly on twigs that are, in most kinds, remarkably long, slender, and supple. A few kinds, such as European crack willow, *Salix fragilis*, and the shrubby goat willow, *S. caprea*, have short and brittle twigs. Bark, smooth on young or bushy trees, develops on larger stems to a fascinating grey-brown network of shallow ribs and fissures.

Willow timber is pinkish-brown, without clear

heartwood, and is exceptionally light in weight when seasoned. Only moderately strong, it has poor natural durability out of doors, though farmers use willow stakes for temporary fences and hurdles. It is a poor firewood. Despite these drawbacks willow is the only wood used for cricket bats in England and much of the British Commonwealth.

Cricket bat willow, the selected variety *coerulea* of white willow, *Salix alba*, is specially grown at wide spacings of 30 feet (9·1 m) on rich, well-watered land in the English lowlands. It forms a handsome tree with a conical crown of blue-green foliage. After about twelve years growth, the trees, which are carefully pruned around their lowest eight feet (2·4 m) to prevent knots forming in their wood, are felled and sawn across into cylinders, about 2½ feet (0·8 m) long. With an axe, a hammer, and wedges, a craftsman then cleaves each cylinder into a number of triangular segments—the future bats. These are carefully seasoned, shaped by hand, compressed, polished and oiled, to make a light bat that will never warp, nor split when the batsman strikes the hard ball. The secret lies in making the 'face' of the bat lie along a radius of the log, where the tough tissues resist penetration.

Other uses of willow timber include wooden shoes, or *sabots*, wooden baskets such as the Sussex trug, parts of artificial limbs and, in days gone by, the shoulder yokes used by milkmaids to carry buckets. Its advantages lie in its light weight, combined with sufficient strength for these tasks.

A remarkable group of willows known as **osiers,** including the common osier, *Salix viminalis*, provide nearly all the material for the baskets made in temperate lands. They are cultivated on good, fertile farmland, with ample water, and the crop is started by planting selected cuttings. Each year the stump of an osier sends up vigorous shoots, often ten feet (3 m) tall, bearing slender leaves. These willow 'wands' are harvested in autumn, and the process can be repeated for many years. A willow wand is a slender cylinder of tough, light wood, which, when it has been moistened, can be woven into any of the intricate patterns needed to make a basket. As it dries it becomes firm, but maintains its resilience. Thin bands for light baskets are made by cleaving a round wand to get three flat strips. If the wands are boiled before their bark is removed, the wood beneath is stained to the typical bright buff colour of many baskets. If the bark is stripped without boiling, white willow results.

With rare exceptions, each willow tree bears only male, or only female, catkins. Both are the oval, fluffy structures often called 'pussy willows' (the name 'catkin' is derived from a Dutch word meaning 'little cat'). On most willows they open in March on the bare twigs before the leaves have opened, and are often gathered as 'palm blossom' for Easter decoration. Male catkins hold many simple flowers, each with two golden stamens. A lot of the pollen is spread by wind, but willow flowers also have nectaries and attract the early bees that carry pollen to female trees. Female flowers each have a single pistil and their general appearance is silvery, not golden. By midsummer they ripen to small, green, oval pods that split and free numerous tiny black seeds, each bearing a tuft of white hairs that aids wind transport. Seeds can only sprout if they land on damp earth within the next few weeks, so wild willows thrive most often on river banks. Each minute seedling

has two oval seed-leaves. Under cultivation willows are always raised from cuttings, which take root readily.

Willow leaves are always simple in structure, without lobes, but they vary in shape from the slender, lance-blades of white willow, weeping willows, and osiers to the broad ovals of goat willows. Leaf margins are often smooth, but sometimes toothed.

Besides the tree and bush forms, there are also willows that send woody stems trailing over the ground. One, the creeping willow, *Salix repens*, helps to stabilize sand dunes. Another, the downy mountain willow, *S. lapponum*, grows on the tundras of the far north, or high up mountains, and also aids soil stabilization in regions of frost and thaw.

Goat willow, *S. caprea*, owes its name to the use of its early spring foliage as fodder for goats. It thrives everywhere on the edges of ponds and patches of wasteland. Crack willow, *S. fragilis*, bears twigs that break off easily, giving a sharp 'crack'. These detached bits readily take root and so help the tree's spread. Not surprisingly, it yields brittle timber. Pollard willows, quaint riverside trees, are lopped to obtain small branch-wood for stakes or basketry, and grow again in mop-headed form.

Walnut and Mulberry

Walnuts were widely cultivated throughout the Mediterranean zone in classical times, and their generic Latin name, *Juglans*, means the nut of the great god Jove, or Jupiter. The specific name of the common European kind, *J. regia*, signifies 'royal'. This valuable nut and timber tree was taken north of the Alps by the conquering Roman legionaries, and when it had become established in England it was called 'walnut', which is derived from words which originally meant 'foreign nut'.

Walnuts develop a bole, or trunk, of great character, stout rather than tall and clothed with a mesh-work of grey bark bearing smooth, silvery ribs. Their twigs are very stout, and carry large, brown, rounded buds, set singly. If you cut a twig across, at an angle, you will see that the large hollow pith is broken into small chambers by thin membranes, a unique feature. The leaves open late, at the beginning of May, and each has a long stalk bearing about seven oval, smooth-edged leaflets, forming a 'compound' leaf. If you crush the leaf, you will at once smell the pungent, pleasant aroma that characterizes this tree. The leaf juice will also stain your fingers brown. Gypsy girls use it to make their faces look sun-tanned,

dark and alluring. In autumn the leaves turn black and fall in broken fragments.

Male catkins, which open in May in groups of two or three, are long, hanging structures made up of numerous flowers, each a group of green bracts and yellow stamens. Their pollen is spread by the wind. Each female catkin is a group of two or three green flowers, set tight on the twig. The female walnut flower has the general shape of an Italian wine flask. The stigma at its tip catches pollen grains, which move down the stem, or style, to the bulbous base, or ovary. This enlarges rapidly and becomes, by July, the green walnut, shaped like a plum. People pluck these unripe walnuts, which have only a soft shell under their green flesh, and pickle them in vinegar.

By October ripening is complete. The green outer flesh has turned leathery and fallen away, revealing the brown, wrinkled nutshell beneath. Crack this, and you will see the curious brown membrane, or septum, that runs across it level with the hard, circular rib that surrounds the whole nut. The brown-skinned, white-fleshed kernel, which extends on either side of the membrane, has a peculiar wrinkled outline. This

Left: In May, walnut expands its compound leaves and opens long, curved male catkins. Flask-shaped female catkins, bearing large stigmas, can be seen in the centre of this picture

Above: When grown in open surroundings, walnut develops a deep, rich-green crown of spreading foliage

Right: In September ripening walnuts resemble large green plums. The flesh falls away later, exposing the pale brown, crinkly shells of the nuts

nutritious and delicious kernel, widely eaten as dessert or in confectionery, is really a pair of seed-leaves. Sow a walnut, and it will send a strong sprout out from its shell, which will draw on the kernel for its supporting food. In the wilds, walnuts are spread by squirrels, and by birds like rooks and jays, who gather the nuts to eat, but drop or hide them in odd places.

Walnut timber is remarkable for its beauty, strength, durability and stability. Within a narrow, outer, cream-coloured sapwood zone, the tree forms heartwood that is, overall, a rich chocolate brown colour, but is shot through with flame-shaped zones of maroon, creamy-brown, or dark grey bordering on black. These lovely colours are revealed wherever the log is sawn through. Because of its high decorative value, walnut is rarely used today for solid furniture. Instead each precious log is sliced repeatedly to yield many sheets of thin veneer, which is applied to cheaper woods, or even to chipboard, to make veneered walnut wardrobes, chests, tables, chairs, beds, radio cabinets and dashboards for luxury cars. Solid walnut, cut mainly from logs too small to yield veneers, is the world's best wood for gun-stocks, because it resists shock and never changes shape. It is also used for tableware like round bowls, and in wood sculpture.

European walnut is widely planted in America, and in fact in all temperate countries, and there are large nut orchards in California and also in Australia. The native American black walnut, *Juglans nigra*, is distinguished by its longer leaves, which bear more numerous, pointed leaflets. Its nuts, though edible, are smaller, and have tough, rough, black shells. Its wood is darker too, a lustrous deep brown, shading through purple to black. It has been highly valued since colonial days for strong, craft-made furniture.

Mulberry trees were introduced from Asia to Europe in classical times, for their delicious fruits, and were given their generic Latin name of *Morus*. There are several kinds. Black mulberry, *Morus nigra*, grows wild in India. White mulberry, *M. alba*, has long been cultivated in China and Japan. These species never make large trees, the tallest being about 20 feet (6·1 m) high and the stoutest only four feet (1·2 m) round. American red mulberry, *Morus rubra*, can grow 70 feet (21·3 m) tall and ten feet (3 m) round. In winter the mulberries are best known by their pinkish-brown bark which becomes thick and rough on old trees. Their buds, set singly on stout twigs, are prominent, oval, pointed and reddish-brown in colour.

Mulberries bear dainty, heart-shaped leaves with toothed edges and a pointed tip. When they open, late in April, they are bright green, but they

become darker during the summer, and turn an attractive, gay, gold shade before falling in October. They are the staple food of the silk-worm (in fact, a caterpillar) and mulberries are extensively grown in the Orient to support the silk industry. The caterpillars feast greedily on freshly picked mulberry leaves, growing steadily larger. In autumn they spin a silken cocoon in which to spend the winter as pupae. Once this is completed, the silk farmer kills the insect, because if it were left to mature as a moth it would bite through the strands of silk when it emerged. Only a few moths are allowed to survive for breeding next year. The fine silk filament is reeled off the cocoons for spinning the silken thread.

Mulberry trees are either male or female. Males are rare in cultivation because they bear no fruit; in their absence the females can ripen edible berries, but the seeds they hold are infertile. Male trees bear, in May, hanging catkins made up of many small, greenish-yellow flowers, each a group of bracts with four stamens to scatter pollen in the wind. Female catkins stand on short stalks and are green, oval bodies compounded of simple flowers, each a cup of bracts holding a pistil bearing two stigmas. As summer advances, the female catkin becomes larger, and fleshy pulp develops round the seed of each flower. The result is a composite fruit which resembles a raspberry. Green at first, it becomes bright pink later and finally red, purple, or white according to the species. All have a fresh, delicious flavour.

Each fleshy portion of the fruit holds a hard

Above: Crimson mulberries ripen in August, amid dark green, heart-shaped leaves with toothed edges

Right: This mulberry tree in the grounds of Tintern Abbey, Monmouthshire, shows a typical bushy form and golden-brown autumn colours

seed, which gives rise to a seedling bearing a pair of oblong seed-leaves, followed by a few oval leaves, and finally by heart-shaped ones. Birds, especially blackbirds, starlings and thrushes, scatter many seeds as they greedily devour the fruit, and in consequence mulberry trees have become naturalized in many districts of both Europe and the North American continent.

Mulberry wood is firm and lustrous, and works to a smooth finish. The heartwood is a rich chocolate brown, with a paler outer sapwood zone. It is used, in America and India, for decorative woodwork, ornaments, turned bowls, and musical instruments.

Elm and Ash

Elms are majestic trees that flourish along hedgerows even better than they do in deep woods. In England they were planted through fertile lowlands during the eighteenth century when old, open fields were enclosed with hawthorn hedges. The kinds usually chosen are able to 'sucker', that is send up fresh plants from their roots, vigorously. When a mature tree is felled, fresh stems spring up from its underground roots, and thrive in the protection of the hedge. The original parent stocks were raised as suckers from one desirable foundation tree. Although there are many kinds of elm, those in one district are often identical with each other, being derived from the same source.

All elms have oval leaves, set singly along twigs. They break out in April, from brown oval buds, between pink bud scales. Each leaf has strongly marked veins, toothed edges, and a pointed tip. A key feature is the elm's uneven, oblique leaf base, either twisted or lop-sided. Delicate pale green at first, the leaves become dark green later, and turn to pale gold before falling in October.

The flowers open in February, well ahead of leaves, in clusters on the bare twigs. From the ground they look like a purplish-crimson haze. Seen more closely, they display five sepals, five purplish-red stamens and a central pistil. Pollination is effected by wind. Fertilized pistils expand rapidly, ripening by May, each small seed lying at the centre of a yellowish-green papery wing, designed for wind transport. The seeds are grouped in dense clusters which are conspicuous above the foliage and are often mistaken for flowers. Many kinds of elm have a low proportion of fertile seed. Others, such as wych elm, shed ample viable seed, but this only sprouts if it

Opposite page: A splendid English elm, growing in a hedgerow, in Dorset, England, shows typical cloud-shaped masses of dark green foliage in midsummer. The same tree is shown on this page, but it has been photographed in autumn, when fading leaves transform it to a tower of gold

alights on moist bare soil in early summer. Each elm seedling has two opposite seed-leaves, then two opposite true leaves, and thereafter normal, solitary leaves.

Elm timber is outstanding for ingrained toughness and resistance to splitting. It is used by craftsmen, in Europe and America, for exacting work where other woods would fail under stress. One example is the hub of a wooden wheel, into which the oak spokes are driven hard to make a tight fit. Another is the seat of a kitchen chair, into which the legs are likewise driven. Mallet heads of elm never shatter under the hardest blow. When cows kick elm cow stalls they do not split. Elm trunks were hollowed out to make water pipes for town supplies and the rim of the larger 'female' end did not break when the tapered 'male' end was driven home to make a watertight joint. Village water pumps, and even the moving part, called the 'bucket', that worked up and down within the upright tube, were carved from elm.

Other leading uses are in rustic furniture, both indoor and open-air, cladding for barns, tough packing-cases for heavy metal goods, the 'bearers' of pallets for fork-lift trucks, and drums for carrying electrical power cables. Elm is also the traditional timber for coffins.

The toughness of elm springs from a peculiar arrangement of pores and associated fibres in its annual rings. These make intricate wavy patterns, and produce a surface figure like the feathers on a partridge's breast. Selected solid elm planks are used to make cocktail cabinets and similar fine furniture displaying this beautiful effect. Elm heartwood is a warm reddish-brown, with a narrow light brown sapwood zone around it. The grey bark is always rough, though its texture varies from one species to another.

In various regions, both in Europe and North America, elms have suffered severely from outbreaks of the Dutch elm disease, so-called because it was first observed in Holland. This disease is caused by a fungus, *Ceratocystis ulmi*, which is carried from tree to tree by a small beetle, of the genus *Scolytus*, which breeds below the bark. The foliage of badly affected trees quickly wilts and the whole tree dies after a few months. Outbreaks have usually occurred at long intervals, but, fortunately, some elms prove resistant and foresters hope to propagate these more widely.

Among the many kinds of elm found in Europe, Asia, and North America, the most majestic is English field elm, *Ulmus procera*, which Constable loved to paint illuminated by sunshine amid the harvest fields in his native Suffolk. The American elm, *U. americana*, makes a magnificent shade tree, traditionally planted beside New England homesteads. Rock elm, *U. thomasii*, native to eastern Canada and the north-eastern United States, shares with the Scots or wych elm, *U. glabra*, of northern Britain, a reputation as an exceptionally strong boat-building timber. Jersey elm from the Channel Islands, *U. carpinifolia* var. *sarniensis*, has a narrow crown like Lombardy poplar, which makes it suitable for street or park planting. The tallest elms are 130 feet (39·6 m) high, the stoutest 21 feet (6·4 m) round.

Ash trees, also common along hedgerows, yield by contrast a timber that splits easily along the grain, yet presents far greater resistance to fracture when used as a hammer handle for a sideways striking blow. The reason lies in its circular pattern of large pores, easily seen as tiny holes on the end of any piece of ash, or as fine grooves on its sides. Between each ring of pores comes a band of very tough, dense summerwood, able to absorb

the force of a hard blow provided its grain has not been cut across. So since the time of the stone age cunning craftsmen have cleft ash logs lengthwise into sections suited to the making of handles, for tools and weapons, and then carved them to their final shape, taking care to leave some grain intact right through each length.

Pick up any striking tool—a hammer, an axe or pickaxe, or any tool which is used under strain, such as a spade or garden fork, and you will find that its handle is cut from ash—or possibly from its only rival, American hickory. Ash is also used for walking sticks and sports goods, particularly hockey sticks, gymnasium bars, oars, golf clubs and tennis rackets, because of its toughness. Ash was always chosen for cart shafts, and also for the 'felloes', the pieces that make up the rim of a

wooden wheel. In warfare, it provided shafts for spears, pikes and lances. Ash is also used for high grade furniture, having an attractive pale brown shade. It is rarely used out of doors, since it has poor natural durability, but it makes splendid firewood.

The tree that yields this uniquely valuable timber is easily recognized in winter by its hard, black buds, always set in pairs except for the one at the tip of each twig. Its ash-grey bark bears shallow ridges and fissures, and its trunk, up to 22 feet (6·7 m) round, bears an open framework of branches up to 148 feet (45·1 m) high. The distinctive compound leaves, which open late in April, are each made up of a long-stalked central mid-rib bearing about seven oval leaflets at its sides. These have shallowly toothed edges and a

pointed tip. Pale or dark green in summer, they turn pale yellow before falling late in October.

The green, catkin-like flowers of ash open in mid-April, ahead of the leaves, in clusters along the twigs. They are wind-pollinated and bear only minute sepals and petals. Each separate flower may be male, with two functional stamens, or female, with one functional pistil, or else it may hold well-developed organs of both sexes. Fertilized pistils develop during summer to become one-seeded fruits, each holding the oval seed at the base of a slender but tough, brown wing with an oval, twisted shape. These fruits are called ash 'keys' from their resemblance to the keys used to unlock mediaeval chests.

Ash seeds are blown everywhere by winter winds, and then lie dormant on the soil for 18 months before sprouting. Each grain then sends up two oblong, opposite seed-leaves, followed by a few oval, simple leaves, then a few leaves with only three leaflets each. A year later the first typical compound leaves appear.

The common ash throughout Europe is *Fraxinus excelsior*, which is an exceptionally hardy tree to be found thriving on northern upland farms. American ash, *F. americana*, is distinguished by its larger and broader leaflets, but is otherwise very similar.

Left: In September, ash ripens bunches of pale brown winged seeds, or 'keys'. Note the compound leaf shown clearly on the left

Left: Ash flowers open on leafless twigs early in May. They may be clusters of male stamens or female pistils or they may hold both sexes. Note the black winter buds

Liquidambar and Tulip Tree

No other tree, not even the maples, can match the autumn glory of the magnificent **liquidambar** tree, *Liquidambar styraciflua* of the family Hamamelidaceae. It originates in the south-eastern United States where it is also called the 'sweet gum' because of a scented resin that oozes from cut stems, and 'satin walnut' from the character of its wood. This attractive, pinkish-brown timber is used for furniture, joinery, toys and tableware, but in Europe the liquidambar is planted solely as an ornamental tree. It thrives throughout southern Europe, and, here and there, on acid soils in the warmer parts of the British Isles.

When mature, liquidambar forms a tall, heavily branched tree, up to 130 feet (39·6 m) high and 20 feet (6·1 m) round in its American homeland. It bears a regularly furrowed, rough, grey bark. A pale brown, corky outgrowth of bark often extends onto its sturdy twigs. The conical buds are set singly at angular bends on these twigs—in contrast to the paired buds of maples.

Liquidambar's palmately lobed leaves, however, closely resemble those of maples. They have long stalks and five to seven oval, pointed lobes that fan out in a star-shaped pattern. Throughout the summer they are dull reddish-green in colour, but in October they virtually burst into flame. They change to blazing hues of pink, orange, scarlet and crimson, often with mauve or purple overtones. Leaves on various parts of the same tree, or even on the same branch, show different colours simultaneously, while the low bright autumn sun augments their brilliance.

Liquidambar's flowers open in April, just before the leaves. Catkins of both sexes are found together on the same tree. Male catkins are hanging, swollen, compound clusters of small flowers that lack petals and are simply groups of stamens which shed pollen on the wind. Female catkins have a more simple design, each being a round

Right: In autumn the star-shaped leaves of liquidambar turn to vivid colours, sometimes totally red but often a mixture of red and yellow

43

head of closely packed flowers hanging on a single stalk. Protruding styles, elongated projections from the ovaries which bear the stigmas, give each catkin a fuzzy appearance. After pollination it ripens into a remarkable brown burr-like fruit, built up of many woody seed pods fused together. The styles project, like spines, at all angles. Eventually the seed pods open and release small winged seeds.

The **tulip tree** was brought to Europe from America around the middle of the seventeenth century, and it was widely planted for its magnificent crown of foliage and remarkable flowers. It is native to the eastern regions of North America,

from Ontario south to Florida. Splendid trees, up to 150 feet (45·7 m) tall and 25 feet (7·6 m) round thrive on the deep rich soils of river valleys—there is a record of one giant 190 feet (57·9 m) tall, and another 600 years old. English records are naturally lower—130 feet (39·6 m) tall and 22 feet (6·7 m) round. In America, this tree is often known as 'yellow poplar', because of its broad fluttering leaves and a similarity in the timbers.

Tulip tree's leaves, which open in May and are pale green in colour, have a very distinctive shape. They stand on long, thin stalks and broaden out into four angular lobes. Instead of a

point at the tip, there is a broad, shallow notch. In autumn these leaves fade to an attractive pale gold, before the winds strip them from the trees. The winter buds, which are set singly along the twigs, have a short but distinct stalk at the base, and then swell out into two thin, pale green bud scales.

The flowers open in June, high in the foliage. They are large, with the general outline of a tulip, but their colour makes them less conspicuous than the tree's name suggests. Each blossom has three green sepals and six broad, cupped petals with recurved tips. They are coloured cream to greenish-white, and bear on their inner surface distinct blotches of orange, which serve to guide pollinating insects towards the nectaries hidden at the base of the flower.

There is a large number of conspicuous stamens bearing long, narrow, bright orange anthers. Within these stands a cluster of green carpels, which do not form a compact female pistil but stand clear of one another. This arrangement shows that the tulip tree stands fairly early in the scheme of plant evolution, for the single, united pistil developed later. As the seeds ripen in autumn, the carpel cluster becomes a brown, narrowly conical fruit. This breaks up gradually, releasing many long-winged seeds, each the product of a single carpel. The seeds sprout the next spring, each sending up two narrow seed-leaves. A group of odd, round juvenile leaves follows, and then the typical broad, notch-tipped leaves.

The bark of the tulip tree is at first smooth and brown, and has a peculiar pungent smell. Later it grows thicker, changes to a dark greyish-brown, and becomes deeply ridged in a strong diagonal network. The timber within has a most unusual colour, being pale greenish-yellow, though the inner heartwood is usually more green than the outer sapwood, which tends towards a clear yellow shade. In England it is known as 'canary wood'. It is used in many countries for making wooden patterns for engineering work, because it is exceptionally stable yet easily cut to required shapes with a smooth, firm finish. In America it is also used for lathe-work, fine joinery, furniture-making and flooring.

The tree's Latin name, *Liriodendron tulipifera*, means 'the lily tree that bears tulips'. Its original American Indian name was *rackiock*.

45

Planes and the Tree of Heaven

Plane trees, known in America as 'sycamores', are readily identified by their broad, lobed leaves, which differ from those of maples or European sycamore in being set *singly* on twigs, never in pairs. If you pull off a leaf, you find at the base of the leaf stalk a deep round socket which fits neatly over a cone-shaped bud. All through the winter this resting bud makes planes easy to name, but most people recognize them by their beautiful, dappled bark, which presents a changing patchwork of white, grey, green, yellow and brown zones and suggests the play of sunlight. Planes regularly shed bark in patches as the outer layers grow older, revealing fresh bark beneath. This habit helps them to thrive in smoky towns, as every tree must breathe through its bark.

The flowers and fruits of planes grow in round clusters on long hanging stalks. These clusters, often called 'bobbles', have earned planes their American nickname of 'buttonwoods'. Each male cluster holds scores of tiny green flowers, and each flower is made up of four anthers on a green base. They open in May, scatter wind-borne pollen, and fall a few weeks later. The similar female clusters have scores of flowers, each consisting of about five clustered pistils, surmounting a ring of four small green petals and four sepals. After pollination they ripen to brown, woody fruit clusters that persist through winter. In spring they break up, releasing tiny brown seeds, each carrying a tuft of hairs which some people find irritating to the skin. These hairs aid the wind dispersal of the seeds. Planes have curious seedlings with slender, recurved seed-leaves, then partially lobed leaves, and, finally, fully lobed ones.

Planes yield a beautiful, firm, strong and even-grained, pinkish-brown timber, prized for the making of high-grade furniture. If it is carefully sawn so as to reveal its network of rays, it shows a lively and handsome figure, and is then called 'lacewood'.

Oriental plane, *Platanus orientalis,* which has deeply lobed leaves with wavy outlines, grows

Left: A magnificent Oriental plane standing beside the lake at Dorchester Agricultural College, Dorset, England

Right: This tall London plane displays the gaily dappled peeling bark, characteristic of the group

wild in Greece and Asia Minor, and is often planted in Italy. **American plane,** *P. occidentalis,* is native through most of the eastern United States. Both these trees were introduced into England at the beginning of the seventeenth century, and somewhere, possibly in the Botanic Garden at Oxford University, a natural hybrid arose in about 1670. This, nowadays called **London plane,** *P.* × *hispanica,* has proved more vigorous and hardy than either parent. It is the favoured street tree of London, Paris, and other European capitals, and is planted on a grand scale in parks, or to shade boulevards. Because it rarely sets fertile seed, the London plane is increased by cuttings or layered shoots, which are low branches pegged to the ground until they take root. Though no tree has yet exceeded 300 years in age, many have reached huge sizes, up to 115 feet (35 m) tall and 27 feet (8·2 m) round.

The popularity of planes as shade and street trees arises from a happy combination of desirable properties. They are vigorous, and can tolerate any amount of lopping. When cut back, they respond by sending forth fresh sturdy shoots. They can therefore be pruned with safety when they grow too big for urban surroundings. Since they are increased from cuttings or layers, every tree is almost identical with its neighbours. The trees of a group or avenue planted at the same time, grow at the same rate with similar patterns of branches and foliage. Coming from a warm climate of dry summers, planes are happier than other trees amid a mass of stone, brick or concrete. The heat reflected from large masonry surfaces does not upset them, and they need only a small circular zone of unpaved ground around their trunks to get air and water to their roots.

Tree of Heaven, *Ailanthus altissima,* rivals the planes as a vigorous shade tree for cities, on both sides of the Atlantic. It originates in China, and its exciting name is a poetic translation of an oriental word meaning 'tree of the skies'. It is easily recognized through its enormous compound leaves, often two feet (0·61 m) long by 18 inches (0·46 m) wide, made up of about 21 separate, short-stalked leaflets. When these leaves open in late April, they are a rich bronze colour, but they soon turn to a lustrous dark green. The mid-rib of each huge leaf looks just like a branch, but it ends in a leaflet, not a bud, and this proves that it is really a leaf-stalk. Each leaflet is oval, and about three inches (76 mm) long. Near its toothed edge it carries curious swollen glands for which no clear purpose has yet been discovered. In autumn the leaflets fall away from the main stalk, which drops later.

Most Trees of Heaven are wholly male or

Left: Deeply lobed leaves and hanging seed balls of the Oriental plane

wholly female. Both types carry large panicles of greenish-white flowers in June or July. Each flower has five or six green sepals, the same number of whitish petals, and a nectary to attract bees. Bees find these flowers a good source of honey and they are not repelled by the flower's strong, acrid scent. Male flowers have ten large, functional stamens, with yellow anthers. Female flowers have small rudimentary stamens, set around a vase-shaped, five-lobed pistil. They ripen by September as large bunches of bright orange-red seeds, which hang like clusters of golden keys high amid the green foliage.

In late autumn the fruit clusters break up, releasing separate small black seeds. Each is carried away on the wind by the twisted, brown papery wing that surrounds it. When the seedling sprouts next spring, it pushes up its wing, then opens two tiny, round, yellow seed-leaves. The first true leaves have only three leaflets, and the normal 'adult' leaves follow.

The Tree of Heaven also spreads vigorously by means of underground roots that send up strong suckers far from the parent tree. It has become naturalized in many parts of southern Europe and the eastern United States, and is now accepted as part of the natural vegetation. In gardens it owes its popularity to its exotic, subtropical appearance. In winter it is easily known through its very stout, greenish-brown shoots, which carry round buds and large, heart-shaped scars where the last year's leaves have fallen. The bark is dark grey to black, and smooth except for wandering pale grey veins running up the trunk. The timber, which resembles ash, has been used for furniture making, but is rarely available commercially. Maximum sizes are 100 feet (30 m) tall and 12 feet (3·7 m) round.

Right: Tree of Heaven grows vigorously, forming a deep crown of huge compound leaves and giving an almost exotic appearance

Rose-tribe trees

Trees that belong to the same botanical group as the garden roses, the family Rosaceae, provide many of the finest displays of blossoms and fruits in forest and garden. All have similar flower patterns, with five green sepals, five showy petals, many stamens with golden anthers, and a central green pistil. All are pollinated by insects, and because they produce abundant nectar many are valued by bee-keepers as sources of honey. In many garden varieties the flowers are double or semi-double, and some kinds are sterile, lacking stamens and pistil. These varieties can be increased only by grafting, and this is a common nursery practice for all the choicer kinds of rose-tribe trees.

The fruits of this group vary widely. Botanists classify the trees into genera according to each type of fruit, which may vary from a cherry to an apple or a hawthorn berry.

Among the **cherry** trees the tallest European wild species is *Prunus avium*, which grows freely in broadleaved woodlands throughout western and southern Europe. In Scotland it is called the gean tree, from an Italian variety of cherry, named *guina*, which was introduced by the courtiers of Mary, Queen of Scots, in the sixteenth century. The gean can become a tall tree up to 102 feet (31·1 m) high, and reach a girth of 15 feet (4·6 m). In gardens and orchards the cultivated kinds of cherries, which are derived from this wild stock, have constantly to be kept in bounds by hard pruning. Some are grown for their luscious fruit, others for their display of blossom.

A cherry tree is easily known by its bark, which is purplish-grey, with a smooth metallic sheen. Running across it are prominent raised bands of brown corky tissue, which are actually breathing pores called lenticels. Sometimes the bark peels away in horizontal strips. Winter buds, set singly along the stout twigs, are large, pointed and oval, and show many outer scales. Flowering branches carry short shoots called spurs, which bear the plump flower buds.

Cherry comes into leaf in late April, expanding an oval, long-stalked blade with a toothed edge and a pointed tip. The leaf is at first bronze-brown, then bright green. Throughout the summer the leaves show mid-green hues, but in autumn they blaze into colour displaying red, orange, and even purple tints before they fall.

The flowering season of cherries ranges, according to variety, from April to late May, so it is possible for tree planters to plan a succession of colour. Wild cherry bears single white flowers, but decorative garden kinds may be pink, red, or mauve, and single or double. Many of these originate in Japan. The wild tree sometimes blooms ahead of its leaves, and its blossoms then look like a snowdrift clothing bare branches.

Cherry fruits ripen quickly and are ready for picking in June and July. Their colours range from white through red and pink to purple and jet black. Each has a tough outer skin, a thick layer of juicy, delicious pulp, and a single hard seed or 'stone'. On wild cherries the pulp is thin, though sweet, and it quickly attracts the birds which scatter the seeds. The seeds lie dormant on the forest floor until the second spring after ripening. When their hard husks split, they send down a little root and raise a short stalk bearing two thick, green, oval seed-leaves. Normal foliage follows.

Cherries yield a beautiful, lustrous brown timber, intricately patterned and shot through with overtones of gold or green. The thin outer sapwood is golden-yellow. The valuable wood of large logs is cut into thin veneers used to ornament high-grade furniture, particularly tables, wardrobes and bedsteads. Smaller pieces are used for solid furniture or for wood sculpture.

The **blackthorn** or **sloe tree**, *Prunus spinosa*, is one of the ancestors of garden plums. It grows wild on woodland fringes and waste places throughout Europe and is often used, like hawthorn, to make a stock-proof hedge. It spreads readily by means of sucker shoots from its underground roots, and forms dense thickets on neglected farmland. Blackthorn is easily known by the black bark of its tough stems

Left: This dainty Japanese cherry, Prunus serrulata, *displays countless pinkish-white flowers in the spring*

(patterned by pale brown breathing pores) and by its sharp spines. The winter buds, set singly, are minute. Some of the smaller twigs are slender and extend the branches by annual growth. Others are short, stout, and bear flowers and fruit. The long-stalked leaves are oval, with toothed edges. They are pale green through summer, and turn golden in autumn.

In April the pretty white flowers open in clusters. They usually expand before the leaves but in those years when the warm spring weather comes earlier they appear amid the delicate greens of unfolding leaves. Each blossom ripens, by October, to a plum-like fruit called a sloe. This has a tough purple outer skin, covered with a greyish-blue shining bloom of wax, which checks water loss. The pale green pulp within is very sour, but sweetens a little after frost. Birds take sloes greedily and scatter the hard brown seed or stone which is at the heart of each fruit. Seeds sprout 18 months after ripening, the tough stone splits, and two stout seed-leaves emerge.

People gather sloes to make jelly, or to flavour sloe gin. The only traditional use of blackthorn's tough, knobbly stems is found in Ireland, where they are used to make a shillelagh, a handy cross between a walking stick and a cudgel.

Hawthorns, which botanically are species of *Crataegus*, such as *C. monogyna*, are aggressive, tough, spiny shrubs that invade wasteland everywhere. They are easily known by the crimson tinge of their grey-brown twigs, and their abundant, sharp spines. Their leaves, which expand from tiny buds in April, have a distinctive wavy outline. Emerald green at first, they soon darken and become reddish-brown before falling

Above: Strong, salt-laden winds from the Atlantic have moulded this coastal hawthorn into its streamlined form

Right: Hawthorn bush laden with its autumn fruits, the crimson haws

in October. The lovely, richly scented blossoms of hawthorns open in May, and the tree is therefore often called the may tree—lending its name to the famous ship *Mayflower* in which the pilgrim fathers reached America. The flowers, borne profusely in bunches, are white, with, in the wild strain, only five petals. Cultivated varieties have red or pink blossoms, single or double in form.

Hawthorn fruits, or haws, are a crimson red, and each carries at its tip five pointed, woody bracts that are remains from the flower's calyx. The yellow pulp is bitter but attracts birds. There may be one, two or three hard stony brown seeds which sprout in the second spring after ripening. Birds spread them everywhere.

Hawthorns are very widely planted, particularly in England, as stock-proof field barriers. A hawthorn hedge needs protection by fences in its early stages, but later becomes remarkably tough and long-lasting. Every few years craftsmen called hedgers cut the hedges back, cutting some stems part-way through in order to bend them and intertwine them with upright stems or new stakes. The hedge is then topped with interlaced hazel rods called 'heathers', and its strength is thus restored. Hedges like these, which can last for centuries, give shelter for cattle, nesting places for birds, and refuges for wild flowers.

The **rowan tree,** *Sorbus aucuparia*, is often called 'mountain ash' because it bears ash-like compound leaves and grows typically on rock faces in the hills. The name 'rowan' is derived from the Scandinavian *raun*. Rowan is frequently planted in gardens because it provides, in a limited space, attractive feathery foliage, which becomes orange-yellow in autumn, besides the bunches of bright, creamy-white flowers in June, and the show of scarlet berries which follows.

Rowans have smooth, purplish-grey bark, and remarkably large, oval, purplish-brown, pointed winter buds, with hairy edges to their scales. Each leaf has about nine leaflets along its mid-rib; these leaflets are oval with deeply toothed edges and end in a pointed tip. The stalks that carry the flowers and berries divide repeatedly, to make a flat head, first of blossom and later of fruit. Rowan berries are too sour to be eaten raw, but when sugar is added they make a tasty jelly. Birds spread them widely. There are several small hard brown seeds in each fruit and these sprout 18 months later. The seedlings have first two seed-leaves, then leaves with a few leaflets, and finally the normal 'adult' form.

Rowan has a cream-coloured sapwood and a strong red-brown heartwood. Logs are so small that it is only used occasionally, usually for tool handles, small furniture and the like. Old superstitions maintain that a rowan tree is a sure guard against witchcraft. To this day rowans are carefully tended beside cottages in the Scottish Highlands to keep evil spirits away.

The **whitebeam tree,** *Sorbus aria*, is only common on chalk and limestone soils. It draws its name from the gleaming white undersides of

its leaves, which are clad in hairs to check the water loss in such dry places. 'Beam' was the Anglo-Saxon word for a tree. Whitebeam leaves, which are oval and pointed with toothed edges, are mid-green in summer and turn pinkish-brown in autumn. Whitebeam's winter buds are large, oval, many-scaled and green, and its bark is smooth and pale grey. The abundant white flowers, which open in June, resemble those of rowan. The berries, too, are similar, but rather larger. The tough, mid-brown heartwood is occasionally used for turned or carved artifacts.

Wild service tree, *Sorbus torminalis*, draws its odd name from its relationship to the 'true' service tree, *S. domestica*, a feathery-foliaged rowan-like tree native to southern Europe. This in turn is called 'service' because the Romans used

its berries to flavour beer, in Latin *cerevisia*. Wild service is a rather rare tree, found sparingly in old woodlands in southern England and Wales, and on the continent. It has lobed leaves like a maple, very pretty flowers like a rowan, pinkish-grey bark broken into squares like a hawthorn, and dull red-brown berries that are just sweet enough to be eaten raw.

The common **crab apple,** *Malus pumila*, is one of the ancestors of the juicy garden kinds. It is called 'crab' from the old Norse word *skrab*, meaning a rough scrubby tree, and in fact it is seldom more. It grows along hedgerows and forest fringes, with a much divided trunk and branches. Its blue-grey bark flakes away, leaving brown patches. Its leaves are oval and pointed, with short stalks and toothed edges. The smaller

Right: Wild crab apple opening its May blossoms in an English hedgerow

Below right: Gay display of pink and white coloured blossom on a cultivated crab apple of a decorative strain

Left: The exquisite white blossoms of wild service tree open in clusters each May, revealing green sepals, white petals, golden stamens and a central pistil. The lobed leaves resemble those of maple

shoots, which bear spines, are of two kinds: long shoots extend growth, while the short shoots, or spurs, bear flowers and fruits. The same plan is found in garden apples, but these are spineless.

The blossoms of crab apple, which open late in April, are white with pink edges and are among the loveliest sights of spring. They ripen, by October, to small, hard, apples with a yellow skin and a pale yellow flesh that is excessively sour. It cannot be eaten raw, but if enough sugar is added it can be made into delicious crab apple jelly. Birds attack the wild fruits as they slowly ripen, and scatter the oval, pointed pips, which have a hard, glossy black outer skin. Little seedling apple trees, each with two seed-leaves, come up the following spring.

The wood of crab apple is reddish-brown, with a cream-coloured outer sapwood. Very tough, it is used for cudgel and mallet heads, or for decorative carving under the name of 'fruit wood'. There is no regular trade, however, and most of it becomes firewood.

Laburnum, Locust and Judas Tree

The gay hanging chains of yellow **laburnum** blossoms, which have earned it the second name of 'golden rain', delight the eye in parks and gardens every May. This small tree, *Laburnum anagyroides*, is native to central and southern Europe. Many exceptionally decorative varieties are cultivated in countries with a temperate climate, and these are increased by grafting.

Laburnum has distinctive, smooth, olive-green bark. The timber within has a narrow creamy-white sapwood zone surrounding a broad core of heartwood which is a deep chocolate brown with an intricate, attractive figure caused by the many small pores. It is hard, strong, durable and stable, but because logs are never large it is only employed for decorative woodwork, such as sculpture, turned bowls, and carved ornaments, and in musical instruments, such as the chanter, which regulates the pitch of Scottish bagpipes.

In winter, laburnum is easily recognized through its dull, greyish-green twigs bearing solitary, oval, pointed buds that have white hairs on the edges of their scales. The dark green leaves set on long stalks, have a compound, trifoliate pattern, each one consisting of three oval leaflets. Laburnum seedlings start life with a pair of seed-leaves, and then bear simple oval leaves before the trifoliate type develops. The leaves turn yellowish-brown before falling in autumn.

The flowers in laburnum's drooping clusters of blossom follow the pattern of its botanical family, the sweet pea tribe or Papilionaceae. Each has five green sepals, enclosing five yellow petals arranged on a peculiar plan. At the top stands a large 'display' petal called the standard. On either side are two smaller petals, known as 'wings' which help to guide a visiting bee towards the lower 'keel', which is built up of two more petals, folded inwards together. The flower holds five stamens with yellow anthers, and a green pistil with a long stigma. At the heart of the flower are nectaries, and to gain honey the bee must force its way past the wings and into the keel. In so doing it carries pollen from the anthers of one flower to the stigma of another.

Following fertilization the green pistil develops into a slender, hard, brownish-black seed pod with a tough skin, and this is ripe by October. It opens with an explosive twist, which throws out the numerous hard, black, tiny seeds within. Laburnum seeds are mildly poisonous, and mischievous children who eat them soon feel sick. They sprout on moist earth the following spring.

Locust also belongs to the sweet pea family and bears flowers like laburnum's, but they are white ones, opening high on the branches each June. A native of North America, locust was given its odd name by early settlers who mistook it for the 'locust', or carob bean, that nourished John the Baptist in the wilderness. Locust's botanical name, *Robinia pseudacacia*, reflects two other common names—'robinia' after Vespasien Robin, the French botanist who introduced it to Paris at the beginning of the seventeenth century, and 'false acacia', because it bears spines like the thorny acacia of the Arabian deserts.

Left: Brilliant hanging chains of laburnum blossom have earned it the more poetic name of golden rain

Right: In June this tall locust or false acacia opens a profusion of white blossoms, all over its tall crown

59

These little spines are set in pairs, and thus provide an easy means of identifying the locust. They are placed on either side of each summer leaf or minute winter leaf-bud. Leaves are ranged singly on tough grey twigs. Locust's branches follow a tortuous course, and though this results in a picturesque crown of foliage, it lessens the value of stems as timber. The main trunk also bends irregularly, and is often lop-sided or fluted. It bears thick grey bark, deeply ridged and furrowed.

The timber has yellow sapwood and beautiful, rich, golden-brown heartwood, with an attractive figure in the grain. It is dense, strong, and tough so that for centuries it was used in America for tool handles, cart shafts and other utensils needing stubborn strength. It is naturally durable, too, and provided fence stakes and gate posts. It is still valued for fine furniture, decorative table-ware, and wood sculpture, though the difficulty of sawing out large, straight planks restricts its general use.

Locust leaves, which open very late, seldom before early May, are pinnately compound. This means that each leaf has a long central stalk, which bears on either side about nine pairs of small, oval leaflets, and ends in a final terminal one. Pale green through spring and summer, these large leaves turn yellow in October and then break up into separate leaflets and stalks when they fall.

Hanging chains of white, fragrant flowers, shaped like sweet pea flowers, open in mid-summer. After pollination by bees, they ripen into long slender black pods, which split in late autumn to release numerous small, hard, black seeds. Locust seedlings start life with two small oval seed-leaves, and then bear a few undivided, oval true leaves. Leaves with three leaflets—like those of laburnum—follow, and eventually the large, compound 'adult' leaf appears.

During the eighteenth century locust was extensively planted on estates in France, Italy, and the neighbouring countries of Europe, but more sparingly in England. The attraction was its excellent timber, well suited to hand work by country craftsmen. It was discovered later that a locust tree, when felled, 'coppices' vigorously, sending up dense clusters of fast-growing shoots from its stumps. Though worthless as timber, these shoots provide good firewood, which can be cropped repeatedly for rural use. Locust also sends up sucker shoots from its underground roots so that once it has been introduced, it is very hard to eradicate. It has been planted on waste land, such as heaps of mine waste, to improve the scenery and check soil erosion.

Vandals who are intent on damaging trees dislike its spiny stems but, if they do cut it back, it quickly grows again.

Locust is particularly suitable for the first afforestation of infertile land because, like other plants of the sweet pea family, it has a special means of increasing soil fertility. Its roots carry nodules which hold a bacterium, called *Bacterium radicis*, which is able to 'fix' the free nitrogen of the air and so create the nitrates and proteins needed for growth. Locusts can grow 90 feet (27·4 m) tall and up to 14 feet (4·3 m) round.

Right: As its leaves unfold in May, Judas tree bears a wealth of purple blossoms directly on its dark branches

Below: Seen close to, locust blossoms, which hang in bunches, resemble sweet peas. The large leaves are composed of many leaflets

An ancient legend declares that Judas Iscariot hanged himself from a branch of a **Judas tree,** after betraying Christ. This beautiful, bushy tree certainly grows in Israel, as well as in many other Mediterranean lands. Botanically, it is *Cercis siliquastrum* of the family Caesalpiniaceae.

People usually recognize the Judas tree by its bluish-green leaves, which are kidney shaped to oval in outline, with no teeth on their edges. Its numerous branches are clad in greenish-grey, smooth bark which becomes darker on the short trunk.

Every spring, in late April, the Judas tree bears a wealth of bright lilac-purple blossoms, which open in short-stalked clusters along the stouter twigs and small branches, though not on the thinner ones. Each separate flower has the general pattern of a laburnum blossom, but with a freer arrangement of the five petals. This gay display, which begins on bare leafless branches and ends amid the bright green of newly-expanding leaves, attracts many pollinating bees. The flowers are sometimes eaten in salads, adding a sharp taste as well as a cheerful colour. The flat black seeds ripen in autumn in broad pods, which are dull red at first, turning brown later.

Judas tree is often grown for decoration in English and American gardens, though it is not hardy enough for northern districts. The American redbud, *Cercis canadensis,* is closely allied to it.

Lime and Horse Chestnut

Lime or **linden trees,** also called basswoods in the United States, grow sparingly in woodlands but are planted everywhere in parks, large gardens and along highways for their graceful form and pleasing foliage. Every leaf has the shape of a conventional or 'playing card' heart, usually symmetrical though sometimes oblique. It has a long stalk, a toothed edge, and a pointed tip. Bright green when it opens in April, it darkens later and changes to a clear gold shade before falling in October.

The tortuous twigs that bear these leaves are usually tinged crimson over their dull green hue, especially on the sides that face the sun. The crimson winter buds, set singly where the twigs bend, show a constant key characteristic: only two bud scales are visible, one larger than another. Lime bark is grey, with a network of shallow ribs. Its inner layer, called bass or bast (from which the American name is derived), is quite exceptionally tough and fibrous. Country-men use it for binding bundles, and it has some historical significance. The open sailing boats in which the early Anglo-Saxon invaders crossed from the continent to England during the fifth century AD had ropes woven from lime tree bast. The Vikings, too, used it for their voyages to Normandy, Iceland, Greenland, and beyond.

Lime flowers open in June, in hanging pale yellowish clusters. Each main flower stalk carries a conspicuous and distinctive, thin, green papery bract which will later turn brown and serve as a wing to help spread the seed. Three or four individual flowers stand on separate shorter stalks arising from the main stalk. Each has five green sepals, five pale yellow petals, numerous stamens with golden anthers, and a central pistil. These flowers smell sweetly to attract bees, who feast on the abundant nectar and carry pollen from tree to tree. Lime is highly valued by bee-keepers as a honey source. Over most of Europe people pick these fragrant flowers and dry them, to infuse them later to make refreshing lime blossom tea. The lime tree is, botanically, a near ally of the tea bush.

Fertilized flowers ripen, by October, to become round woody 'boxes' which hold from one to three hard seeds. The seed sprouts the next

Left: Yellowish-white flowers of lime arise in clusters on a long stalk that also bears a papery bract

Right: Common lime makes a splendid parkland tree, spreading its foliage right down to the level at which cattle browse

spring, sending up two fingered seed-leaves, oddly shaped like an open hand, and then bearing typical foliage. The commonest lime in cultivation, known in Europe as the common lime, *Tilia × vulgaris*, is a hybrid, chosen for vigour, which rarely sets fertile seed and is therefore increased by cuttings. Its parents are the large-leaved lime, *T. platyphyllos*, and the small-leaved lime, *T. cordata*, both native to Europe, including Britain. Lime is England's tallest broadleaved tree, reaching 154 feet (46·9 m) at Duncombe Park in Yorkshire, and girths may be up to 22 feet (6·7 m). The leading North American native species is the American basswood, *T. americana*, common throughout the eastern United States.

Lime timber is an even pale brown colour. It is not particularly strong or durable out of doors, but it is firm, stable, and easily carved to precise shapes, with a smooth finish. It has therefore become the sculptor's wood, and was always used by Grinling Gibbons, the English master, for his intricate seventeenth century displays of flowers, fruits and feathered fowls. The same properties ensure its use for shoe lasts, hat blocks, and piano keys (since it keeps a true shape below the ivory surface).

Common lime is a favourite tree for planting in stately avenues or as a feature in a broad park, but it has two defects. One is a habit of sending out dense bushes of twigs near ground level. The other is its profusion of 'honey dew', actually an excretion made by tiny aphides that suck the leaf sap but do not fully digest it. This sticky, sugary liquid falls in minute drops onto chairs, tables or parked cars. A mould fungus then turns it a dirty black. The beautiful silver-leaved lime, *T. petiolaris*, from south-east Europe, has neither fault, and should be planted in preference.

Horse chestnut owes its peculiar name to the Turks, who used its nuts to cure broken-winded horses. An extract of its bark is still employed in veterinary medicine. Surprisingly, this handsome tree remained unknown in western Europe until 1557 when the Italian botanist Pierandrea Mattioli encountered it in Istanbul. It was introduced to Vienna by Charles de Lécluse in 1576, and has since been spread throughout Europe and North America and indeed to every temperate country where people wish to see a magnificent show of tree blossom.

The huge, distinctive leaf of horse chestnut is palmately compound, being built up of five to nine leaflets that fan out from a main stalk like the fingers of a hand. Each leaflet broadens out from its base, then narrows abruptly to a broad tip. It has strong veins and a slightly toothed

Left: In autumn the tough spiky husk of the horse chestnut splits and reveals the glossy, round, dark brown nut within. Note the large compound leaf, with radiating oval leaflets

Far left: The pink horse chestnut, a garden hybrid, bears spikes of beautiful, rose-coloured blossoms

Left: Horse chestnuts' winter buds break in spring. Sticky brown scales fall away, and big compound leaves emerge from amid greyish-brown down

edge. Deep green in colour, it turns to rusty brown before falling and breaking up in October.

The leaves and young shoots spring from the well-known 'sticky buds', large oval structures set in pairs along the stout twigs and clad in a resin that becomes clammy in spring. The leaves then unfold amid a coating of pale brown woolly hairs, probably a protection against water loss. When a leaf falls it leaves a horse-shoe shaped scar, bearing 'horse-shoe nails' that are actually the sealed-off ends of main veins. The reddish-brown bark forms squarish plates that flake away from old trees. Horse chestnut timber is a pale creamy brown, and is soft and weak. It is occasionally used for toys or trays, but most goes for firewood.

Horse chestnut's splendid display of blossom opens in May, when spikes bearing around 20 short-stalked flowers expand above its foliage. Each flower has five green sepals, five large white petals bearing pinkish-brown or yellow honey-guide markings, five curved stamens, and a central pistil. Its uneven shape, with larger lower petals, obliges a visiting bee, seeking nectar, to crawl up over the pollen-bearing anthers and the stigma of the pistil, so ensuring pollination.

Each pistil develops into a large nut with a spiny green husk which shatters when the nut falls after ripening in October. The horse chestnut within has an irregular oval shape, and a shining bright brown skin. There is a pale brown oval patch on one side, which has earned these trees their apt American name of 'buckeye'. The pale yellow flesh of the nut is bitter, and the only creatures that eat it readily are deer. Fallen nuts that sprout next spring send up sturdy shoots, bearing typical compound leaves from the outset.

The common white horse chestnut, *Aesculus hippocastanum*, is native to Asia Minor, Albania and Greece. Widely planted as an avenue and ornamental tree in streets, parks and gardens, it can reach 125 feet (38·1 m) in height, and a girth of 21 feet (6·4 m). The pink horse chestnut, *A.* × *carnea*, which is increased by grafting on the common stock, is a nurseryman's hybrid between the white kind and the American red buckeye, *A. pavia*. Yellow-flowered horse chestnuts, such as *A. sylvatica*, the painted buckeye, grow wild in America but are rarely seen in Europe.

Below: In May this magnificent horse chestnut displays candles of white blossom all over its spreading crown

Maples and European Sycamore

Maples are a well-known group of forest trees found across Europe, Asia and America. They form the genus *Acer* in the botanical family Aceraceae. Key characteristics are the placement of buds *in pairs*, except at twig tips, and broad-bladed, winged seeds which are likewise in pairs and which twirl round like the blades of a helicopter when they fall. The tallest European kind is the great maple, *Acer pseudoplatanus*, which in England is called 'sycamore'. It is often planted in America, where the true native sycamore is actually a plane of the genus *Platanus*.

Nearly all maples bear the characteristic palmately lobed leaf that has become familiar on the national flag of Canada. Bright green when they open in April, these leaves darken later, and in autumn they suddenly blaze into fantastic displays of scarlet, gold and orange, before the first wintry winds sweep them away.

In spring, just as the buds are about to open their oval, pink scales, there is a sudden uprush of sweet sap towards the branches. The starchy food reserves that have been stored in roots and trunk are mobilized to promote fresh growth by transformation into maple sugar dissolved in sap. Now, as the snow thaws, the Canadian or New England farmer who owns a 'sugar bush' starts his tapping. He drives a metal spout into each tree trunk, and sets a cup beneath it to catch the sap that flows out. Daily he collects buckets of sap, and takes them to his boiling house, where a big metal pan is set over a wood fire. Boiling concentrates the sap into rich, sweet maple syrup or tasty, brown maple sugar. It must be done the same day, otherwise the sap will ferment and turn sour. Maple sugar sweetened the food of the early American settlers and remains among the favourite national sweetmeats.

Maples yield a firm, pale brown timber which, though not durable out of doors, is valued for many remarkable indoor purposes. It makes the hardest, smoothest and most durable floors, and is therefore chosen for ballrooms. It can be carved to fine outlines that hold intact despite repeated wear, and it never stains food or textiles. These properties ensure its use for wooden rollers in textile mills, dairy and kitchen utensils including butter pats that imprint a design on soft butter, parts of shoes, shoe lasts and shoe trees, bobbins for thread, toys, and wooden printer's type for large letters. In North America large quantities of small logs are used for paper pulp, and it is everywhere a good firewood.

Maple or sycamore wood is chosen for the back, sides and stock of violins and similar stringed instruments, though the belly must be made of more resonant spruce wood.

The wavy 'fiddle-back' figure to be found in the grain of exceptional sycamore logs is greatly admired for its lively play of light and shade. It is used for radio cabinets, car dashboards, and luxury furniture. Many veneers can be cut from one good stout log, and selected trees have changed hands for considerable sums of money. Trees with this figure in their grain are identified by cutting a 'window' in the bark to view the rippling grain below. Maple used in the solid form is also an attractive furniture timber, and antique chairs and tables made in Europe, or by American craftsmen in colonial days, fetch high prices.

European sycamore can be distinguished from most other maples by its oval green buds and the rounded lobes of its dark green leaves. These turn pale brown when they fade, and lack the brilliance of other maples. The flowers open in May, in long-stalked hanging bunches, with only the central flowers of each bunch fully developed. Others remain only male or only female. Each perfect flower has a short stalk, five green sepals, five yellowish white petals, eight stamens and a central pistil with two stigmas. Pollination is effected by bees and other flying insects.

Sycamore fruits ripen in October, in pairs having an angle of about 90 degrees between their wings. Each brown seed holds a peculiar seedling, ready to sprout, with the two strap-shaped seed-leaves already bright green. The wind blows these abundant seeds to all sorts of odd places, such as gutters and alleyways between buildings where they sprout vigorously next spring. The first true

Above: When grown in open surroundings European sycamore develops a deep, dome-shaped crown. A hardy tree, it is often planted to shelter mountain farmsteads

Above right: Sycamore flowers, which open in May, are grouped in long hanging bunches. Note the lobed leaves

Right: The paired winged seeds of sycamore, borne profusely in autumn, hang down in colourful clusters

leaves are oval and pointed, and the lobed leaves follow later.

Sycamore is not native to Britain, but its vigorous reproductive powers have enabled it, since its introduction by monastery gardeners in the Middle Ages, to become naturalized, and it thrives like a native tree. Its distinctive grey bark, smooth at first, develops irregular flakes later, which break off, leaving brownish patches. Records for height are 110 feet (33·5 m), and for girth 23 feet (7 m) round. Sycamore is widely planted both as a specimen tree for its lovely crown of foliage and as a source of valuable timber.

Norway maple, *Acer platanoides*, native to Scandinavia and most European mountain ranges, is a smaller tree that has also been introduced, mainly for ornament, to Britain and America. It can be distinguished by small pointed red buds on thin reddish-brown twigs, sharply pointed, angularly lobed leaves, and seeds that have the wings of each pair in a straight line, not at an angle. Unlike most other maples, it flowers in March, before the leaves open. Upright clusters of blossoms, all well developed, burst from the bare twigs in a gay display of bright yellow, tinged with green. The Norway maple's autumn tints are bright yellow to orange, and these attractive

Above: Norway maple enlivens dull March days by opening bunches of bright golden blossoms on bare stems

Left: In Britain's National Arboretum at Westonbirt, Gloucestershire, Japanese maples make a brilliant display of leaf colours every autumn

features, combined with a shapely habit, make it a favourite tree for street and park planting. The reddish-brown bark is thin, with shallow fissures.

For centuries Japanese gardeners have cultivated exceptionally beautiful strains of two native maples: *Acer palmatum* and *A. japonicum*. These varieties, increased by grafting, are now widely grown in European and American gardens. Most of the named cultivars are low bushes that thrive best on acid soils in the partial shade of taller trees. Some, like 'Osakazuki', excel in the brilliant scarlet of their autumn leaf colour. Others like 'Dissectum' or 'Atropurpureum', bear very finely divided, bronze-crimson leaves that resemble a delicate lace.

In the eastern United States and in eastern Canada the commonest species is the **sugar maple,** *A. saccharum*, also called the rock or hard maple. This tree bears clusters of long-stalked flowers that open with the leaves and it shows colourful red and yellow autumn foliage. Another common, attractive kind is the **silver maple,** *A. saccharinum*, which has elegantly divided leaves with toothed edges, green above but gleaming silver below. It is often planted in Europe as an unusual specimen tree.

Evergreen broadleaved trees

Most broadleaved trees in the world's temperate countries lose their leaves when winter approaches because they cannot draw water, essential for active life, from cold or frozen soil. But certain countries have what the geographers call a Mediterranean climate, with mild, wet winters and hot, dry summers. These include, besides the lands bordering the Mediterranean Sea: Portugal, California, the southern tip of South Africa, and much of south-west and south-east Australia. In these places a remarkable group of broadleaved trees has developed and adapted to the climate. The leaves are evergreen, so they enable the trees to grow while rainfall is plentiful during mild winters. They are also thick and tough, with glossy surfaces coated with a wax that checks water loss during the hot, dry summers. Each evergreen leaf lasts for three or four years and then, during autumn, turns dull brown and falls.

Evergreen broadleaved trees and shrubs have been extensively planted outside their natural homelands because they give shelter and ornament at a dull, cold time of year. The British Isles are fortunate in having mild winters, due to the Gulf Stream, a warm current flowing across the Atlantic, that enable many Italian and Californian woody plants to thrive. But others fail because they are not fully hardy under prolonged winter frosts.

Holly, *Ilex aquifolium*, is the hardiest of this group. It is native to western Europe as far north

Left: As winter approaches, holly ripens clusters of bright crimson berries, set amid glossy, dark green, spiky foliage

as Scotland, but cannot grow in the colder east. The allied American holly, *Ilex opaca*, grows in the southern and eastern United States from New York to Texas. Holly leaves, set singly along the dull green twigs, are glossy and dark green above and pale green beneath. Their basically oval shape is distorted on all the lower branches by twists that end in angles with sharp points, and the tip is pointed too. This spiky armour protects the foliage from browsing animals who would otherwise eat all the lower holly leaves when other green fodder was scarce. Higher up, beyond the reach of cattle or deer, spineless oval leaves are usually found.

The flowers of holly open in May in clusters in the leaf axils. Each tree is either male or female, and male trees bear no berries. Fortunately, nurserymen, who increase selected kinds of holly by grafting, can guarantee the sex of each variety. Flowers of either sex have four white waxy petals, and nectaries to reward the bees that carry the pollen. On a male tree each flower holds four stamens, while on a female tree there is a single four-lobed ovary in each blossom.

On female trees bright red berries ripen in December, just in time for sprays to be gathered for Christmas decoration. By tradition, the prickly, evergreen, berry-studded foliage symbolizes Christ's crown of thorns, the blood shed at his passion, and his promise of eternal life. In woods and along hedgerows the berries are plucked by the birds, particularly thrushes, that

spread the seeds. After lying dormant in the soil for 15 months, the seed sprouts in spring, bearing two soft deciduous seed-leaves before the tough prickly, true leaves develop.

Holly bark is steel grey and smooth. The wood is nearly white in colour, dense, hard and smooth, and is used for decorative carving and furniture. A first-rate firewood, it burns without previous seasoning, while the waxy foliage flares like a torch in any forest fire. Many decorative strains of holly, some with very prickly leaves and others variegated with yellow, silver or red, are cultivated in gardens.

Eucalyptus trees, also called gum trees, are native only to Australia, but have been introduced to many Mediterranean and subtropical countries with frost-free winters. They are grown on a large scale for timber, paper pulp and firewood in South and East Africa, South America, California, India, Spain, Portugal and southern Italy, as well as for ornament. The kind illustrated here is the Tasmanian cider gum, *Eucalyptus gunnii*, which proves hardy in mild coastal districts of the British Isles, such as Cornwall.

A constant feature of the many kinds of eucalyptus is their bluish-green, waxy leaf. The wax coating checks water loss, but makes foliage dangerously inflammable in forest fires. Young trees bear semi-circular juvenile leaves that clasp the stem in pairs. Adult trees hang their slender leaves sideways on drooping twigs. This lessens evaporation by letting hot rays from the sun pass

through the foliage, which consequently gives
little shade. The leaves hold strong-smelling
eucalyptus oil, which is distilled commercially for
use in perfumery and cough cures. Eucalyptus
trees grow very fast to great sizes—300 foot
(91·5 m) giants in Australia are the world's tallest
broadleaved trees. Their bark is smooth and grey,
but flakes off in strips to give a dappled effect,
with warm brown and pale yellow patches. Some
kinds yield good, pale brown timbers, used for
firewood, joinery and furniture.

The flowers, which appear in abundant clusters
in spring, are at first capped by a round bud-scale
which falls off later. Each has a basal green disc,
a 'powder-puff' cluster of yellow or red stamens,
a central pistil and ample nectaries. Eucalyptus
flowers are a major source for the honey made by
bees in Australia. The seeds, which ripen in
autumn in small green conical pods, are small
and hard. Each little seedling bears two deciduous
seed-leaves followed by evergreen juvenile foliage.

Box, *Buxus sempervirens,* grows abundantly
as a shrub or small tree on limestone hills throughout southern Europe and very locally in southern
England, notably at Box Hill in Surrey. Its neat
foliage of paired, oval, mid-green leaves is
familiar through its use as neatly trimmed, low
garden hedges. Although it never grows more
than 30 feet (9·1 m) tall or exceeds two feet
(0·6 m) in girth, it yields a valued timber—bright
yellowish-brown, smooth, strong, dense, and
hard-wearing. This is used for rulers, mathe-
matical, surgical and musical instruments, the
finest wood sculpture, kitchen utensils and wood
engraving blocks for printing.

The small green flowers open in clusters amid
the leaves in May, both sexes growing on the
same tree. Each male flower holds four green

petals and four stamens. Pollination is effected
by wind. Each female flower has four petals and
an ovary with three stigmas. It ripens, by October,
as a papery, horned capsule holding many little
black seeds. Seedlings bear two oblong deciduous
seed-leaves, then normal evergreen foliage. The
grey bark of box, smooth at first, develops a
pattern of neat regular squares.

Sweet bay, *Laurus nobilis,* is a commonly
cultivated evergreen shrub, or, in Italy and neighbouring lands, a tall, rugged tree. It is widely
grown for ornament in Britain and America,
though it is not fully hardy in the north. Sweet
bay is known at once by its dark, almost blackish-
green, glossy, oval, pointed leaves, which have
slightly toothed edges. If you crush them you
can smell immediately the piquant fragrance that
accounts for their use as a spice by every good
cook. You may find a leaf, too, in tins of
Portuguese sardines.

Bay trees can stand close clipping and training,
and thrive when grown in large pots, even in
smoky towns. Their foliage provided ceremonial
crowns for the victors of games in classical times,
and also for poets and musicians—hence the
term Poet Laureate for the person appointed as
poet to British Royalty.

In June, bay bears clusters of small flowers
amidst its dark foliage. Each tree is male or
female. Flowers of both sexes are alike in having
four sepals, four yellowish-white petals, and
nectaries since they are insect-pollinated. A male
flower has twelve stamens, while a female flower
holds instead a single pistil. This ripens, by
October, to a one-seeded, juicy, black berry. Bay
berries are sour, but birds devour them and
spread the seeds. The name 'bay' comes from
French *baie,* meaning berry.

73

Small broadleaved trees

There is a fascinating group of small trees, which, although they never grow large enough to yield timber, add interest and beauty to hedgerows and forest fringes. Some have gay flowers, others bright berries that make good winter food for birds. They all provide low cover and nesting places for wildlife. Some play a part in soil conservation, or in the spread of the forest, through the intermediate stage of scrub, on to bare land or worn-out pastures. Many have quaint traditional uses in rural life.

Spindle-tree is so called because its smooth, white wood appears to have been preferred since prehistoric times for making the old-fashioned spindles that peasant women twirl by hand, to spin woollen thread. It forms a bush or small tree with greyish-green foliage, easily recognized because its young, dark green stems have a *square* cross section, unique among trees. The finer twigs are also green, but round. They bear, in opposite pairs, long oval leaves with toothed edges and pointed tips, which arise from small, green, pointed winter buds. In autumn the leaves turn to pretty shades of yellow and pinkish-brown, but they soon fall.

Spindle-tree's small, greenish-white flowers open in clusters in leaf axils in June. Each flower has four sepals, four petals, and nectaries to attract insects. Flowers may be male, with four stamens, or female with a four-celled pistil, or possibly hermaphrodite, having organs of both sexes. Female pistils ripen, by autumn, into a remarkably attractive four-lobed fruit pod, that changes from greyish-green to bright pink, both inside and out. When they split, they reveal four hard black seeds hidden within a fleshy coating that is coloured bright orange. Though poisonous to humans, spindle berries are harmless to the birds that attack them and spread the seeds.

Common spindle, whose berries are often gathered from hedgerows for decoration, is *Euonymus europaeus* of the family Celastraceae. A southern European kind, the broadleaved spindle, *E. latifolius*, is cultivated in English and American gardens for its larger, more showy fruits.

Purging buckthorn owes its odd name to the fact that its glossy black berries are a strong purgative, long used in herbal medicine. The 'buckthorn' was originally 'buck's horn'. Among

Left: Early in autumn spindle tree ripens pretty, four-lobed pink berries, amidst red-brown autumn foliage. Note the orange seed-coats

Above: The pretty berries of alder buckthorn ripen from white to pink and black. Oval leaves develop warm autumn colours

its foliage you can find short shoots, bearing corrugations, that look surprisingly like the rugged horns of a buck roe deer. Other shoots are long and slender, extending the length of the branches. Still others are modified into thin spines that discourage browsing sheep.

Purging buckthorn grows on lime-rich soils, making a shrub or small tree with rough, grey bark. Its pale green leaves, oval with toothed edges, are set in pairs and have a bluntly pointed tip. Small green flowers open in May in leaf axils. They lack petals, and have only four sepals to attract the insects that spread the pollen. Male flowers have four stamens. Female flowers, on a separate tree, hold a four-celled pistil that ripens, by autumn, to a glossy black berry. Botanically, purging buckthorn is *Rhamnus carthartica* of the family Rhamnaceae.

Alder buckthorn is a pretty little tree which grows in woodland swamps over most of Europe, including southern Britain. It only attracts attention in autumn, when its small, oval, opposite leaves become a pleasing pale gold colour. It is called 'alder' because it thrives in swamps amid tall alder trees, and a 'buckthorn' because it is allied botanically to purging buckthorn. Its fine, black twigs, which bear grey breathing pores, are actually spineless. The botanical name is *Frangula*

Right: Purging buckthorn has neat oval leaves and clusters of glossy black berries, which hold a powerful purgative

75

alnus, family Rhamnaceae. Alder buckthorn bears, in May, small greenish-yellow flowers that are followed, in October, by bunches of juicy berries that change from green, through red, to black.

The German name of *Pulverholz*, meaning 'gunpowder wood', gives a clue to alder buckthorn's unique economic value. Charcoal made from its small stems, which have dark grey bark, yellow sapwood, and a red-brown heart, yields the best gunpowder known. When heated in an enclosed kiln, the wood breaks down into an even-grained black charcoal, which, when mixed with the right quantities of sulphur and saltpetre, gives either a reliable explosive or a slow-burning substance. Its most important application is in slow fuses for firing charges of explosives, including land mines and blasting charges. These delayed-action devices must burn at predetermined rates of so many feet a minute to allow their firers time to get clear. Hence this quaint little tree has been an ally of the mining engineer, and also a precious munition of war.

Alder buckthorn bark holds a powerful purgative, which has been extracted commercially as a substitute for cascara. The latter medicine is in fact derived from a closely allied Californian tree, *Rhamnus purshiana*.

Dogwood forms a small, bushy tree that grows rampantly on lime-rich soil, especially the chalk downs of southern England. Its name is derived from the use of its thin stems, which have a hard white, horny-textured wood, as 'dags' or skewers, and not from any association with dogs. It is easily recognized by its blood-red stems which bear paired oval, pointed leaves. These are dull green in summer, with a hint of red, but turn crimson in autumn. In June, dogwood opens its bunches of pretty, white, waxy flowers, each holding four green sepals, four white petals, four stamens and a two-celled pistil. These blossoms attract bees by their nectar and their faint, pleasant scent.

Dogwood berries ripen in autumn in conspicuous clusters on the red twigs and foliage. They are glossy black and each holds a single, hard black seed. Birds eat them greedily, digest the pulp, and void the seed. As a result dogwood thickets spring up everywhere on abandoned pastures. If they are cut back, fresh shoots spring up from underground roots, so this pretty shrub has become the despair of conservationists trying to maintain grassy nature reserves on chalk downs. Only sheep, who bite back its regrowth, can hold it in check.

Botanically, dogwood is *Cornus sanguinea*, meaning 'the blood-red horny-wooded tree', of the family Cornaceae.

Elder forms a straggling bush or a low tree that grows around odd places like rubbish heaps, farmyard dunghills, badger burrows and rabbit warrens, as well as in woodland clearings, for it thrives best on soil rich in nitrogen. Its seeds get carried to such places by birds that swallow its pulpy berries and void the hard black seeds on ground enriched by their droppings.

Large elder stems have a thick, pale brown bark which is fibrous and soft. This attracts wild badgers and domestic cats, who scratch it to clean their claws. The wood within is white, hard and strong. It is sometimes used to make toothpicks or fine probes used by watchmakers to clean delicate mechanisms.

By contrast the bark on thin elder twigs is greyish brown and smooth, except for the pale pores. These small twigs are brittle, because their

centre is filled with very soft, light, white pith. If this is hollowed out, a twig can be made into a pea-shooter, or even a whistle. The pith itself is used by botanists to hold specimens, such as thick leaves, which would otherwise be difficult to cut into thin sections. The pith holds them firm while they are sliced with a razor to yield transparent sections to be mounted on slides for examination under a microscope.

Elder twigs bear paired leafy buds which start to change from purple to green early in spring. In April they expand to become long-stalked compound leaves, made up of about three pairs of opposite leaflets and one terminal one. Leaflets are oval, with toothed edges and a pointed tip. They fade from pale green to yellow in autumn.

In June, elder opens showy umbels or clusters of white blossoms with a distinctive musky scent. There are scores of flowers in a single multi-stalked head. Each has five small sepals, five petals, five stamens and a three-celled pistil. Pollination is effected by insects. Elder flowers are sometimes used to flavour cakes or wines, or to make elder-flower water for cosmetics.

By September the flower heads have matured to become clusters of purplish-black berries, which wandering birds soon strip from the trees. They are edible, but taste insipid if eaten raw. Country folk bake them in elderberry pies, or ferment them with sugar to make elderberry wine.

Common elder is *Sambucus nigra* of the family Caprifoliaceae. The similar American elder, *S. canadensis*, bears blue berries.

Tamarisks form spreading bushes or low trees that grow wild along seacoasts and on inland sand dunes in southern Europe, North Africa, and western Asia. They are planted in similar places and also in gardens in Britain and America. The word 'tamarisk' comes from Hebrew *tamaris*, meaning a sweeping broom. Their branches and leaves resemble those of cypresses and heaths, a pattern that lessens water loss in dry places. Tamarisks are also naturally tolerant of salt and will grow on exposed sea beaches.

Tamarisk's tough woody stems bear chocolate brown bark with paler pores. Bark is smooth on

Right: On the wild Guelder rose only the small central flowers of each group are fertile. Large white flowers on the group's rim are sterile, but help in attracting insects

young branches but gets rougher and furrowed with age. The fine twigs are pinkish to reddish-brown, and divide into narrow green twiglets. Both twigs and their finer divisions bear many narrow, scale-like green leaves, often overlapping. In autumn the foliage turns yellow and the finer twiglets break away. Some kinds are evergreen and retain dark green scale-leaves through the winter.

In June tamarisk opens myriads of pretty pink flowers, in long dense spikes. Each tiny blossom has four to five sepals and an equal number of petals, four to five stamens, and a three-celled pistil. In autumn minute seeds, each with a tuft of hairs, are released from the small seed pods.

The commonest species in gardens is the four-stamened tamarisk, *Tamarix tetrandra*, introduced from the Caucasus. It bears its catkin-like flower-heads on the wood of the previous year. The French tamarisk, *T. gallica*, grows wild on the coasts of western Europe. It has five stamens in each flower, and bears panicles of blossoms on the young shoots of the current year. Both belong to the tamarisk family or Tamaricaceae.

Guelder rose is found in two forms. The graceful natural kind grows in moist woodlands and is occasionally cultivated in gardens. It is a shrub or small tree with brown bark and spreading

Below: In autumn, wild Guelder rose ripens drooping bunches of bright red berries, which gleam like jewels in the sun and are often translucent

three-lobed leaves, set in pairs, which assume rich orange-gold tints in autumn. Wild Guelder rose displays broad flower-heads in June, and a curious feature is that only the inner flowers of each head, or umbel, are fertile. These effective flowers have five small green sepals, five small greenish-white petals, five stamens and a pistil, with nectaries to reward visiting insects. These insects are attracted to the flower head by the much showier sterile flowers of the outer ring. These consist simply of five sepals and five large white petals. Lacking stamens and a pistil, they can neither shed pollen nor ripen seed.

Around the beginning of the sixteenth century, a peculiar form of this shrub was discovered in Guelderland, nowadays part of Holland, and this accounts for the odd name of this tree, which is not a rose at all. In this variety *all* the flowers are sterile, so it cannot set seed and would eventually die out in the wilds. Nurserymen, however, increase it by layering—bending down the branches into the soil until they take root. It bears remarkably effective round heads of white blossoms, which have gained it the popular name of 'snowball tree'. Botanically it is the variety *sterilis* of the wild species *Viburnum opulus*, family Caprifoliaceae.

The fertile variety bears, in October, remarkably beautiful hanging bunches of translucent red berries, which have ripened from the inner fertile flowers of each head. They glow like gems in the autumn sun. Each holds a single hard brown seed. They are too sour for people to eat, but birds relish them in midwinter and so spread the seeds.

Wayfaring tree, *Viburnum lantana*, is closely related to Guelder rose but grows in a different habitat, thriving only on dry chalk downs or limestone hills. Its odd name was bestowed by the poetic botanist Gerard in 1597 because he found it common along wayside hedgerows. Before that it was called 'hoar withy'—'withy' because its twigs are pliant like those of willow, and 'hoar' from its coating of white hairs. This felty covering enables the wayfaring tree to avoid excessive water loss in its dry home.

In winter the wayfaring tree is easily known by its naked buds. These have no scales and each future leaf and flower can be seen already formed, only the hairy down protects them. Buds and leaves grow in opposite pairs. In spring, the leaves expand to oval, wrinkled blades, always greyish-green and woolly. Clusters of pretty white flowers open in June—each has five sepals, five petals, five stamens and a two- or three-celled pistil.

In September the gay berries ripen from green

through scarlet to black, often displaying three colours together. People are tempted to pluck them for indoor decoration but they quickly decay, sending out an odour of rotten fruit. Birds, however, enjoy eating their pulp, and spread the single hard black seeds they hold.

The **cercidiphyllum,** or katsura tree of Japan and China, is best known in Europe and America by the Latin name of *Cercidiphyllum japonicum* (family Cercidiphyllaceae). In the Orient it forms a stately tree, up to 120 feet (36·6 m) tall, and yields a firm timber that is valued for the most intricate artistic carving. Elsewhere it is grown only for ornament, and in Britain it seldom becomes more than a bush. Cercidiphyllum bears male and female flowers on separate trees. Both are inconspicuous, lacking sepals and petals. They spring from woody spurs and open before the leaves; pollination is effected by wind. The female flowers ripen later to pods holding winged seeds.

The bluish-green leaves of cercidiphyllum are set in pairs, and have a characteristic kidney-shaped to heart-shaped outline. The tree's attraction as a garden ornament lies partly in its neat shape, but mainly in its vivid autumn colours, varying from brown through bronze to orange and red.

Above: Foliage and multi-coloured fruits (white, red and black) of wayfaring tree

Above right: Cercidiphyllum or katsura tree, Cercidiphyllum japonicum, is cultivated in gardens for its gay autumn foliage

Right: Wild privet bears spikes of pretty, white, scented blossoms above paired, glossy, dark green leaves

Privet is best known as a rather dull, almost indestructible, hedging shrub which survives the smoke and grime of great cities. In such places it is repeatedly clipped back to keep it in shape, and never bears flowers or seeds. The species grown for hedging is *Ligustrum ovalifolium* from Japan; it is propagated by cuttings. If it is abandoned and left to grow tall, however, it becomes an irregular bushy tree, up to 20 feet (6·1 m) high, with a thin, pale brown bark and a very hard, white timber. In May this free-growing privet bears spikes of creamy-white flowers with a strong heavy scent that attracts visiting insects. Each individual flower has four green sepals, four petals, two stamens and a central pistil. In autumn bunches of black, one-seeded berries succeed the flowers.

An allied shrub, also a member of the olive family or Oleaceae, is the wild European privet, *Ligustrum vulgare*. This flourishes on limestone soils, including chalk downs in the south of England. It differs from the garden race in having more open sprays of leaves, which are only half evergreen. They change from dark green to reddish-brown in midwinter, and then fall. The white flowers grow in loose spikes and are followed by rather open spikes of large, black juicy berries, attractive to birds.

The Pines

The true pine trees are described here as a representative botanical genus among the conifers, or cone-bearing trees. This group as a whole is distinguished from the broadleaved trees by several constant features. They ripen their seeds in a woody cone or, in a few exceptional cases, a fleshy berry. These seeds develop on the surface of the scales that make up the cone or berry, and when it ripens the scales open and the seeds fall out. In most conifers the seeds have thin wings and are carried away by the wind. The seedlings that sprout from the seeds have, in most cases, a bunch of numerous seed-leaves, though in a few species there are only two or three.

Cones develop from small, soft, bud-like female flowers which, after pollination, gradually become large, hard, brown and woody. The male flowers that provide pollen grow separately, though nearly always on the same tree. They resemble catkins and are built up of many yellow stamens that shed golden pollen, usually in spring. This pollen is always carried to female flowers by wind, never by insects.

Leaves of conifers are, with few exceptions, shaped like needles, being long, narrow, and usually tough. In some kinds, such as cypresses, these needles clasp and hide the twigs. In others, like the monkey puzzle tree, they are broad and scale-like. In others again, like the swamp cypress, they form feathery fronds. This needle shape reduces water loss, and enables conifers to grow in colder and drier places than broadleaved trees. Because of it, they are sometimes called 'needle-leaved trees'. Nearly all conifers are evergreen, and each needle lives through three or four winters before it falls. In America a common name for the group is, therefore, 'evergreens'.

The timber of conifers has heartwood and sapwood, and annual rings made up of light springwood and darker, heavier, summerwood, just like the timber of broadleaved trees. But in most kinds it is markedly softer, and conifers are therefore called *softwoods*, whereas broadleaved trees are, to the timber trade, *hardwoods*. Coniferous softwood has a simple structure, being made up mainly of long water-conducting 'tracheid' cells, also called fibres. These make it very suitable for papermaking, in processes that break down the wood into its fibres, then felt them together as a tough, thin, pliable sheet. Coniferous timber is easily worked, and as it has reasonable strength it is universally preferred for ordinary building construction, packaging, and box making. It also provides the bulk of the world's transmission poles, mine props, and fencing. It makes good chipboard, hardboard and blockboard, also plywood and cardboard.

Coniferous forests are a world economic resource of immense value, supporting huge sawmills and paper mills. The largest forests stretch across northern Europe and Asia, and across North America from the Pacific to the Atlantic. Other important ones stand on the mountains of Europe, including the Alps, and on the hill ranges of the United States.

Most conifers hold a remarkable substance called resin, which occurs in special cells through the timber, bark, needles, buds, cones and even certain seeds. Resin is a mixture of fragrant turpentine and wax-like rosin, which seals wounds and checks attacks by insects or fungi. In Spain, Portugal, south-west France, and the southern United States, pine trees are tapped to harvest this resin or 'naval stores', which is used in paints, varnishes, printers inks, and quick-drying treatments for printing papers. Rosin is also an essential coating for every violin bow.

All the conifers are often loosely referred to as 'pines' or 'firs', but to the botanist, gardener, forester, and lumber merchant, each group is very distinct. 'True' pines of the genus *Pinus* have an easily recognized key characteristic. After their first year of life as seedlings, during which they bear solitary needles, they always have evergreen needles grouped in *twos, threes, or fives*. This number is constant for each kind of pine.

The growth of pines is remarkably regular. Each spring a large bud at the tip of each stem bursts and releases a fresh green shoot that grows one foot (30 cm), two feet (61 cm) or even, in

Tall Scots pines in the English Lake District, displaying characteristic, rounded, irregular crowns

California or Florida, six feet (1·8 m) longer, all in a few weeks. Growth in shoot length then stops for the year. As the shoot elongates, needles open in small groups all along it. Side branches only develop from the terminal bud cluster formed each year.

Male flowers of pines open in May on shoots already one year old. They are pretty clusters of yellow stamens that scatter abundant, golden, wind-borne pollen. Female flowers open in an unusual position, at the very tips of newly expanded shoots. Each is a little red globe, made up of many scales, yet smaller than a pea. It receives wind-borne pollen but does not develop fully in its first year. Instead it becomes brown and hard, enlarges to about pea size, and so passes its first winter. Next spring it enlarges rapidly, becomes soft and green, and takes on the shape of the final cone, peculiar to its species. In the second winter, its scales again become hard, brown and woody. Later, in its second spring, the scales open in dry weather and the seeds, two from each scale, drift away on the wind.

A typical pine seed has an oval, white kernel in a hard brown seed coat, firmly fixed to an oval, brown, papery wing. When it sprouts on damp earth, it puts out a small, pinkish-white root which bends its stalk and lifts the main seed up in the air. The seed coat then splits and falls off, releasing a tuft of about twenty needle-shaped seed-leaves. From the centre of this a shoot emerges, bearing solitary needles rather like blades of grass. In its second year, and always thereafter, the young pine tree bears needles grouped in twos, threes or fives.

Pine timber is resinous, with well-marked dark orange-brown summerwood bands and paler yellowish-brown springwood zones. Its heartwood holds more resin than its sapwood and is darker throughout. Pine has only moderate durability out of doors, but is easily treated with standard preservatives. Strength and hardness vary with species, being satisfactory, though moderate, in all two-needled pines. Most three-needled pines, including American pitch pines, are hard and make, for example, long-wearing floorboards. By contrast, five-needled pines are soft; the Swiss stone pine, *Pinus cembra*, is used for carving toys, while the North American white pine, *P. strobus*, provides an attractive, easily worked wood for joinery and interior trim.

Overall, pines are a major source of general purpose timbers for industry and agriculture throughout their natural range—the temperate regions of the Northern Hemisphere. Species that grow well in subtropical climates have been introduced to new countries, notably in Australia, New Zealand, South America, and South, East and West Africa, because they produce commercial lumber and paper pulp faster than any native tree. Despite their resinous character, pines are a major source of raw material for making paper and rayon textiles.

The most common two-needled pine throughout Europe is that known in Britain as **Scots pine,** *Pinus sylvestris*. It has a vast geographic range from Spain to Siberia, and from the Scottish Highlands and Norway to Turkey. In America and Canada it is grown as an ornamental tree or, surprisingly, on a large commercial scale as a Christmas tree. Scots pine is easily recognized by its relatively short—one to two inches (25 to 51 mm)—blue-green twisted needles, set in pairs. Its buds are red-brown and end in a blunt, convex point.

Young, thin stems have grey bark, but this soon flakes away, and reveals a lovely, thin, orange-red bark that is a sure means of identification, as well as a bold and attractive feature, long appreciated by landscape painters. It gleams in the sun, high amid the tree's crown of blue-green foliage. This crown becomes irregular with age, resembling that of a broadleaved tree rather than a conifer. The bark near the base of a Scots pine's trunk becomes thicker, and soon divides into pinkish-grey plates, separated by a network of dark grey fissures. The remarkable colours of bud and bark have earned this pine the name, in both French and German, of 'red pine'. In the British timber trade, its red heartwood gives it the name of 'Baltic redwood', since most is imported.

Scots pine cones have a distinct shape, being truly conical or only slightly asymmetric. They are grey in colour and each scale bears a dull brown swelling called an umbo.

In the Scottish Highlands this pine grows to

Left: Male flowers of Scots pine open in yellow clusters along upright expanding shoots. Female flowers, left, are tiny red globes, always at shoot tips

great size and age. In 1954, a tree felled in the Queen's Forest of Ballochbuie, near Balmoral Castle, in Scotland had 300 annual rings, which meant that it was a sapling in the reign of Charles II. A stem 24 feet (7·3 m) round has been measured at Guisachan (a Gaelic name meaning 'little pine wood') in Glen Affric Forest, Scotland. The British height record for Scots pine, 120 feet (36·6 m), is held by a tree at Oakley Park in Shropshire. Scots pine is widely planted in British and Irish woodlands, even though lodgepole pine, *P. contorta*, introduced from Oregon and British Columbia, exceeds it in speed of growth.

Corsican pine is a fine example of Europe's 'black pines', the *Pinus nigra* group, in which it ranks as variety *maritima*. The Canadian yellow pine, *P. resinosa*, also called Norway pine, found in eastern Canada and New England, has similar characteristics. The European pines of this group are called 'black' because they lack the red shades of Scots pine. Their thick, fibrous, much-fissured bark is a uniform grey. The needles are dark, sage-green, without a hint of blue. In many varieties the needles are straight, but in Corsican pine they are long and flexible, bending gracefully to form a tassel of foliage. The distinctive buds are blunt at the base, but taper suddenly to a sharp point. The cones are distinctly larger than

Right: Corsican pine always maintains a well-balanced, symmetrical crown of branches and foliage

those of Scots pine, and are a brighter brownish-grey, with a glossier umbo (a protuberance like the boss on a shield) on each scale. They have a broad base and are always oblique or lop-sided in shape, one side being larger than the other.

On the island of Corsica this pine forms magnificent forests, holding trees 400 years old, 160 feet (48·8 m) high, and up to 16 feet (4·9 m) in girth. The timber, available in broad planks, resembles that of Scots pine, but tends to be paler with less heartwood, and with less strength. Growth is fast, and Corsican pine has been widely planted in central and southern England, and even in Scotland and Wales, although only in favoured districts with much sun and little rain. It exceeds native Scots pine in height, reaching 147 feet (44·8 m), but the greatest girth is only 14½ feet (4·4 m).

Other varieties of *Pinus nigra* are important timber trees in Spain, France, the Swiss and Austrian Alps, the Apennine mountains of Italy, and in Turkey. With a more southerly distribution, and notably in Portugal, Spain, the Landes region near Bordeaux in south-west France, the Maritime Alps, and the coastal lowlands of Italy, Corsica and Sardinia, the **maritime pine,** *Pinus pinaster*, is the leading timber tree. This has long, leathery needles set in pairs, buds

with reflexed scales, reddish-grey, much divided bark and huge cylindrical brown cones. It is often tapped for resin, obtained by shaving off thin layers of wood from living trees, each successive spring.

Stone pine, *Pinus pinea*, is a hardy, storm-firm tree which grows along the Mediterranean coasts of Spain, France and Italy, and develops a remarkable, flat crown of foliage. Hence it is often called 'umbrella pine'. Though long-lived, the stone pine never grows to any great heights; 80 feet (24·4 m), with a girth of 20 feet (6·1 m), is the maximum. Its tough, dark green needles are grouped in pairs, and the buds have reflexed scales.

The cones take three years to ripen and are exceptionally large, six inches (152 mm) long by four inches (102 mm) wide. Cone scales, tough and woody, are each 1½ inches (38 mm) long by ¾ inch (19 mm) wide. Two seeds, or 'stones', are borne on each scale, making around 100 in each cone. A stone pine seed is about ¾ inch (19 mm) long, flat on one side and convex on the other. It has a strong, purplish-brown seed coat and an edible white kernel that is both nutritious and delicious. The wing is only rudimentary, a papery scale less than ¼ inch (6·3 mm) long. Clearly, stone pine depends for its spread on man, seed-

86

eating animals and birds, rather than on the wind.

Stone pine is the source of the *pignons, pinocchi,* or pine kernels that are widely used by confectioners to make cakes and sweetmeats, and by vegetarians as a staple food, either raw or roasted. In the groves tended for this harvest the pines must be spaced far apart so that each tree gets ample sun, soil and moisture. As an ornamental tree, stone pine is often planted in the milder parts of Britain and North America, and also in South Africa and Australia.

On the Monterey Peninsula of southern California grows a rare, remarkable pine, aptly called the **Monterey pine,** *Pinus radiata.* It braves the fierce salt-laden gales from the Pacific Ocean. Its dark brown bark is immensely thick and rugged, with deep fissures. The needles, which are borne in threes, are a bright emerald green and rather soft. Cones are large, six by four inches (152 mm

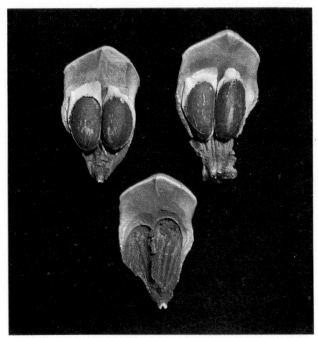

by 102 mm), brownish-grey and oblique, and they often grow in clusters. The seeds are oval, with a black skin, and are $\frac{1}{4}$ inch (6·3 mm) long. They carry a well-developed pale brown wing, one inch (25 mm) long. An odd feature, which Monterey pine shares with some other American species, is that cones do not open fully when ripe. Instead they persist on the branches for many years, releasing a few seeds each spring. This delayed release increases the tree's chances of successful reproduction.

Monterey pine is valued in America only as a picturesque coastline tree, not as a timber producer. In the British Isles, where it only succeeds in the mildest districts, it plays a similar role. A tree at Cuffnells, in Hampshire's New Forest, may be taller than any in California; it is 140 feet (46·7 m) tall. Another at Bicton in Devon measures 22 feet (6·7 m) round.

In several countries with Mediterranean or even subtropical climates, including Spain, southern Italy, North Africa, South Africa, Australia, New Zealand, Chile and Argentina, Monterey pine has become a timber tree of the highest economic value, the mainstay of huge sawmilling and paper-making industries. Rapid growth, up to 9 feet (2·7 m) in height each year, is the secret of its widespread success.

Bristle-cone pine, *Pinus aristata,* a five-needled kind, is so named because each scale on its cylindrical cone bears a little prickle. It is also called fox-tail pine because of its brush-shaped foliage. It grows high in the arid mountainous areas of Colorado, Utah, Nevada, Arizona and south-east California, forming a small tree rarely more than 40 feet (12·2 m) tall. Bristle-cone pine attracted little attention until archaeologists, while seeking to date the habitations of native

Indians from pieces of worked wood which had been preserved in dry ruins, started to count the annual rings of recently felled trees. To their amazement they found some of the oldest living trees on earth, with over 4,000 annual rings, visible under the microscope, in each small stem. Here we have a tree older even than the mighty sequoias of California.

Because bristle-cone pine forms wider rings than usual in occasional wet summers, the researchers were able to build up a pattern of local rainfall over thousands of years. They could then fit the details of the wooden artefacts into this plan, so establishing dates for the Indian cultures they were studying.

Larches and Old-World Cedars

Larches are the only common conifers that lose their leaves in winter. Most of them originate on high mountain slopes where the winter cold is too prolonged for any tree to retain its leaves all the year round. In consequence, larches are easily known by the soft texture of their needles, designed for only one season of active life. Except on the youngest or 'long' shoots, which bear solitary needles, the needles of larches are grouped in pretty rosettes around a woody knob, technically a 'short' shoot. These knobs persist for many years, so even in winter they are an easily recognizable feature for all larches, that is, trees of the *Larix* genus. Between the knobs the long shoots, leafless after their first year, carry curious long smooth scales. On winter twigs the resting buds are conspicuous; they have brown scales and are large and pointed at shoot tips, small and rounded elsewhere.

Common or **European larch,** *Larix decidua,* grows mainly on the higher slopes of the Alps, below the zone of dwarf, mountain-pasture vegetation, and also high on the Apennines and the main ranges of central Europe. In the British Isles and lowland Europe it has been widely grown. since the eighteenth century, as a timber tree.

In America it is cultivated only for ornament. In April the breaking tufts of bright emerald green needles on the larch twigs provide one of the gayest sights of spring. These needles become a duller green later and change, in October, to vivid orange-yellow before they fall. The bark of young twigs is pale yellow or straw-coloured.

Male flowers open along with the leaves in April, forming groups of golden stamens that shed abundant, yellow, wind-borne pollen. At the same time the female flowers open on the same tree. They are usually a warm pink, but occasionally white. Their rosette-like shape has earned them the title of 'larch roses'. During the ensuing summer they ripen rapidly to become oval or barrel-shaped brown, woody cones, with blunt or hollow tips. Beneath each of the blunt, straight, thin scales two seeds develop, each an oval brown grain with a triangular wing. Cones ripen in the autumn following pollination. Seeds are only released gradually, and most are spread later by dry, spring winds. Each larch seedling has a tuft of about six seed-leaves, then solitary needles. Knobs bearing needle rosettes do not appear until the second year.

Larches develop a thick, fibrous, grey bark

Right: Larch bears flowers on bare twigs in April. Male flowers form yellow clusters and female flowers are oval, crimson-purple rosettes

broken by distinct fissures in a net-like pattern. As befits a tree designed to face the blizzards, thunderstorms, and avalanches of the high Alps, larch yields a tough timber, 25 per cent stronger than other conifers. Its heartwood, which is coloured red-brown like terracotta, is naturally durable, even in contact with the ground. The sapwood is pale yellow. In the highlands of Europe, larch is applied to the most demanding constructional uses, including the building of bridges, farmsteads, houses and fencing. In the British Isles larch is preferred for gates and fences, including panels for garden boundaries, and repairs to farm buildings and cottages. An important, specialized use is for the planking of the hulls of wooden fishing boats.

Japanese larch, *Larix kaempferi,* forms huge forests on the slopes of the mountains of Japan, and is abundant on sacred, snow-capped Mount Fuji. It was introduced to Europe in the mid-nineteenth century, and planted extensively when foresters discovered it grows faster than the European kind. Japanese larch has reddish-brown twigs, blue-green needles, and reflexed scales on its short round cones, which look like rosettes. Early in the present century a hybrid between European and Japanese larches was discovered on the Duke of Atholl's estate at Dunkeld, Perthshire, Scotland. This **Dunkeld larch,** *Larix eurolepis,* shows hybrid vigour and grows faster than either parent. It is now bred deliberately in seed orchards, planted with alternate rows of European and Japanese parent trees, to promote cross-pollination. Growth records for larches in Britain are: European, 146 feet (44·5 m) tall and 19 feet (5·8 m) round; Japanese, 120 feet (36·6 m) tall, 9 feet (2·7 m) round; hybrid or Dunkeld

larch, 101 feet (30·8 m) tall, 8 feet (2·4 m) round.

The commonest larch in Canada and the northern United States is the **tamarack,** *Larix laricina,* also known by its Red Indian name of *hackmatack.* It is distinguished by relatively few, broad scales on more open cones. An important commercial timber, its lumber is used for railway sleepers or ties, poles, posts, piling, boxes, crates, boat-building and pulpwood.

The **cedar of Lebanon,** *Cedrus libani,* has captured man's imagination ever since Solomon, King of Israel, bought huge quantities of its timber from Hiram, King of Tyre, to build his famous temple in Jerusalem, as related in the First Book of Kings and the Second Book of Chronicles. To all the peoples of the sun-scorched, treeless lowlands of the Middle East, there was something miraculous about the magnificent forests of fragrant evergreens flourishing on the high snowy mountains in Lebanon, 6,000 feet (1,830 m) above the Mediterranean Sea. These splendid conifers are adapted to living through hot, dry summers and making good use of winter rainfall. They flower in autumn, and two years later release from their large, barrel-shaped cones the winged seeds that will sprout when winter rain or snow moistens the soil. Cedars are widely grown as ornamental trees in Europe and America, for their obvious and exceptional beauty.

Many trees with fragrant foliage or scented wood are called 'cedar'. The old-world, or true cedars of the genus *Cedrus* are easily known by their dark, tough, evergreen needles grouped around short shoots. These shoots elongate very slowly year by year, and bear scars where past needles have fallen. On long shoots, which

Left: Cedars of Lebanon, seen here on their native mountains, spread magnificent, broad, level crowns of mid-green foliage

extend growth, the needles are solitary. Male flowers, which open in September, are club-shaped, and scatter golden wind-borne pollen. Female flowers, green and bud-shaped at first, expand slowly through two summers to become woody, swollen, purplish-brown cones with hollow tips. Their scales, which are very broad, eventually fall away, leaving a central stalk. The oval seeds below them have triangular wings and when they sprout they bear about ten deciduous seed-leaves, then solitary needles, and finally needles grouped on short shoots.

Cedar bark is dark grey, rough, and broken into numerous small, irregular square patches by shallow fissures. The timber has a dark brown heartwood, which is naturally durable, and a pale brown sapwood zone. It is fragrant through-out with cedarwood oil, strong, yet easily worked. An odd feature is that its annual rings never make true circles, but have wavy edges. Where cedar timber is plentiful, as in the Himalayas, it is used for house, farm, and shipbuilding, and even for railway sleepers or ties. Where it is scarce, most of it goes for decorative use, in solid furniture or for veneer, fine joinery or ornaments.

Cedar of Lebanon's most striking character-istic is its level spread of branches in flat planes, which makes it highly desirable as a landscape feature. Though rarely a tall tree—England's tallest, in the New Forest of Hampshire, scales only 120 feet (36·6 m)—it can reach impressive girths, up to 27 feet (8·2 m) at Blenheim Park near Oxford.

Three other cedars grow in the cool air of high mountains in the northern subtropics, isolated by hot semi-desert wastes. All are often seen in cultivation as decorative trees. The one with the widest range is the **Indian cedar,** *Cedrus deodara,* or deodar tree of the Himalayas. Its eastern name means 'the gift of God'. Deodar, a major timber producer in its native highlands, is best distinguished from the others by its gracefully drooping branch tips. On the high Troodos Mountains of Cyprus grows the **Cyprus cedar,** *C. brevifolia,* easily recognized by its short needles. Its forests provide timber and, as in the Lebanon, form a major tourist attraction.

On the snowy Atlas Mountains of Algeria and Morocco grows the **Atlas cedar,** *C. atlantica,* one of the few African conifers. This is distinguished by its fine ascending branches, which make an acute angle with the upright trunk. Its blue form, variety *glauca,* bears needles with a marked waxy bloom, a device which limits water loss beneath the glaring sun at high altitudes. This variety, which is increased by grafting on to a common cedar stock, is one of the most beautiful conifers in cultivation. It is hardy and vigorous, and flourishes on dry chalk or limestone soils where few evergreens can thrive.

Spruces and Silver Firs

Spruces are the characteristic conifers of the north and the high mountain ranges farther south. The key feature that enables anyone to name them at once is the presence of a little peg at the base of each needle. These needles are always set singly along the scaly twigs, and are inserted all round them on upright or drooping shoots, but on horizontal shoots they lie in two flat ranks on either side, like a herring-bone. If you pull a green, living needle, it will tear away from the twig, bringing its basal peg with it. But if it dies naturally, after its evergreen life of three or four years, it leaves the peg behind. Hence the older leafless twigs of all spruces are rough to the touch, being studded with dead pegs —an unmistakable feature.

As spruce stems get older and thicker, the pegs gradually disappear from the bark, which remains fairly thin throughout the tree's life. The trunk is often buttressed at the base. It tapers evenly upwards and spruce trees are nearly always beautifully symmetrical, especially where they stand in the open. Their branches droop gracefully to form a cone-shaped, pointed crown. During each successive spring, growth is extended by brown winter buds. These burst and release a rapidly expanding shoot that bears soft, bright green needles, already developed within the sleeping bud.

Spruce shoots, unlike those of pines, often bear small side shoots. The presence of the resulting small knots, between clusters of larger knots, is a useful clue—well known to lumbermen—for identifying spruce timber, no matter how it may have been manufactured later on.

In May the spruces open oval clusters of male flowers at intervals along their side shoots. These flowers are generally crimson or yellow in colour, and shed golden, wind-borne pollen. Small, bud-like female flowers, coloured crimson, violet or purple, appear at shoot tips. After pollination, these mature rapidly during one summer to become brown woody cones, cylindrical in general shape. They hang downwards, in contrast to the upright cones of silver firs.

Cones ripen, and may be gathered for seed supplies, in autumn. If left on the tree, they open their scales next spring and release, from each scale, two brown winged seeds. The seed is oval, and so is its papery wing. When a seedling sprouts, it unfolds a rosette of about 20 seed-leaves from within its husk. Typical peg-based needles follow.

The timbers of all the spruces are remarkably consistent throughout the log. Both the heartwood and the sapwood are very pale yellowish-white. The timber trades of many countries term this lumber 'whitewood'. The thin summerwood zone of each annual ring is pale brown. None of the wood is naturally durable out of doors, nor is it easy to treat with preservatives. Its strength is only moderate. Yet spruce wood has many virtues—it is easily worked by hand and machine tools, light in weight, strong enough for most indoor purposes, consistent in colour and texture, and available in great quantity. Spruce has therefore become the leading timber in all northern countries for flooring and roofing, joinery and interior trim, packing cases and wooden boxes of all kinds, kitchen furniture, and also for less exacting outdoor uses such as fencing and sheds.

Spruce is the finest timber in the world for papermaking. Its long, thin, conductive cells break down under mechanical or chemical treatments to become flat, ribbon-shaped fibres that felt together into an ideal, strong, smooth-surfaced web of thin tissue. Springwood fibres are flexible, and the proportions of stiffer summerwood fibres and troublesome resin are low. Little or no bleaching is needed to get the paper white enough for newsprint.

Spruce is also very adaptable to all kinds of mechanical and chemical processes that need wood as their raw material. It makes good chipboard, hardboard and laminated board, and peels well into veneers for plywood. If it is ground fine, it makes colourless wood flour used as face powder or as a filler for plastics. Chemically treated, it yields the pure cellulose that is the basis for rayon or 'artificial silk' textiles, transparent cellophane wrappers, and

the woods of certain kinds, even under the microscope.

Despite this similarity, each species, and even each local variety of spruce is finely adjusted to the climate of a particular region. The gardener raising ornamental trees can grow most kinds in most temperate climates, but the forester aiming at profitable timber production must make a careful choice of his seed source.

The common spruce throughout Europe, *Picea abies,* carries the English name of **Norway spruce,** because it was introduced to Britain from Scandinavia at the beginning of the sixteenth century. This is the stately tree that flourishes in vast forests right across northern Europe, and on all the high mountain ranges such as the Alps, the Apennines, the Carpathians, and the Pyrenees. Its thin bark has a distinct reddish tinge, which explains its Italian name of *abete rosso* and its German one of *Rottanne.* Its rich, deep green foliage is built up of flat, rather soft needles, each ending in a blunt point. The distinctive cones are deep brown, around four inches long by one inch across (101 mm by 25 mm), and cylindrical. They have flat, triangular scales and always droop from the twigs. They have become familiar as the pattern for the weights used on Swiss cuckoo clocks. In all its

Left: Norway spruce thrives on high mountains, bearing loads of glistening snow all winter on its shapely conical crown

even nitro-cellulose explosives. Spruce in some form enters every home, more or less every day, disguised as a newspaper, a food wrapper, or a fabric.

The enormous spruce forests of Canada, the northern United States, Scandinavia, Russia, and the mountain ranges of Europe form an economic asset essential to modern civilization. Today they are tended by expert foresters to ensure perpetual supplies to huge sawmilling, papermaking and cellulose chemical industries.

Spruce gets its name through two by-products, once imported to England from Prussia (the name of 'Pruce', meaning Prussia, was altered to 'Spruce'). One was spruce leather, made by using its bark to tan hides. The other was spruce beer, flavoured with its sharp-tasting foliage. In Britain spruce is widely known as the 'Christmas tree', because it has been the favourite evergreen for displaying lights and gifts ever since 1840, when Prince Albert introduced this custom from his native Germany to the royal household. The Latin name *Picea* is linked to pitch, a black tarry waterproof substance once obtained by tapping spruce trunks.

Botanists and foresters recognize over 30 different kinds of spruces. Most are very alike, however, and the timber expert cannot distinguish

Left: The long, slender, brown cone of Norway spruce hangs downwards from twigs that bear dark green needles set on tiny pegs

Above: Sitka spruce, from Alaska, has pale brown cones with crinkly scales. Its sharply pointed needles are bluish-green or silver

native forests, Norway spruce regenerates freely from wind-spread seed. In the British Isles where it must, in practice, be raised artificially, it holds a firm place as a timber producer in every large forest or woodland estate. British records for height and girth are 156 feet (47·5 m) tall and 14 feet (4·3 m) round. In Germany spruce may attain 200 feet (61 m) in height, and 18 feet (5·5 m) in girth.

Across Canada and in the north-eastern United States the commonest spruces are **white spruce,** *P. glauca,* and **black spruce,** *P. mariana.* In the eastern part of their range they share the ground with the **red spruce,** *P. rubens.* All these have small cones, around one inch (25 mm) long, and can only be told apart by small differences in the colours of their twigs and foliage, as their names suggest. Taken together their forests form a vast reserve of timber and pulpwood, though none becomes a really big tree.

Along the Pacific seaboard of North America from Alaska to California grows the **Sitka spruce,** *P. sitchensis,* named after the former Russian colony of Sitka, on Baranof Island off southern Alaska. This spruce is easily recognized by its silvery blue-green needles which end in a sharp point. Its short, oval cones are pale brown, with distinctive crinkly scales and minute winged seeds

below them. Largest of the spruces, Sitka may reach 200 feet (61 m) in British Columbia, by 36 feet (11 m) round. Its forests support big saw-mills and paper mills using logs transported by coastal shipping.

Because it is adapted to regions with high annual rainfall, spread all round the year, Sitka spruce has proved outstanding throughout the main afforestation regions of Scotland, Ireland, Wales, and northern England, where it is planted in greater numbers than any other tree. It grows upright in the face of the fiercest salt-laden Atlantic gales. British records are 175 feet (53·3 m) high and 25 feet (7·6 m) round.

By contrast, the **blue spruce,** *P. pungens,* and its even bluer variety *glauca,* are adapted to the arid climate of the Colorado desert. Their bluish-green sharp-pointed needles owe their colour to a wax that checks water loss under a blazing sun. They never grow fast, but are widely planted as ornamental evergreens throughout the warm zones of America and Europe, including the British Isles.

Li-kiang spruce, *P. likiangensis,* which comes from Szechwan in China, is often cultivated in parks and gardens as a small decorative tree. Its attractive needles are bi-coloured—dark green above, silvery with wax below. Conspicuous

95

Above: Flowering twig of Li-Kiang spruce, Picea likiangensis from China. Male flowers form crimson clusters which disperse golden pollen. The upright, red, female flowers ripen later to form purple cones

Left: Colorado blue spruce makes a fine ornamental tree, with a symmetrical crown of silvery-blue foliage

crimson male flowers open in spring, and the pretty red female flowers develop into purplish-brown cones by autumn.

The name **silver fir** has been adopted for the evergreen conifers that comprise the genus *Abies*, because the commonest European species, *Abies alba*, is called *sapin argenté* in French, *Weisstanne* in German and *abete bianco* in Italian. All these names mean 'silver' or 'white fir' and arise because the undersides of its needles bear two silvery white bands of wax. These bands restrict water loss during critical spells of hot, dry, or cold weather. In America these *Abies* conifers are called 'true firs'.

Silver firs have a similar needle pattern to the spruces. The needles spread all round upright or drooping shoots, but form two or four flat ranks, in a herring-bone pattern, on level shoots. There are no pegs at the needle bases, however, and if you pull one away it leaves a flat, circular scar.

Both male and female flowers of silver firs resemble those of spruces, but their cones are quite different. These cones develop rapidly from wind-pollinated green female flowers to become, by late summer, conspicuous green, upright cylinders composed of many scales with a bract, or smaller scale, below each one. Around September, the scales and bracts turn brown and

woody. A few weeks later the whole cone 'shatters' or breaks up. The scales and bracts fall away, and release, from below each scale, two large oval seeds—each with a triangular papery wing. All that remains on the twig is the cone's thin, upright central axis, which persists through the winter.

The seeds sprout on the forest floor next spring. A peculiar feature of the silver fir seedling is its manner of forming two circles of seed-leaves, one long, one much shorter. There are about ten slender leaves in each ring. The next upright shoot bears normal needles all round it and flat foliage develops on the first side shoots.

Silver firs develop rather thin, grey bark, smooth on some species, but broken into irregular squares on others. The buds at twig tips are usually blunt and resinous. Resin blisters often develop on the bark of small branches, and if these are broken, they exude a clear yellow, sweet-smelling resin often called balsam. Hence the group is often known in North America, as 'balsam firs' or simply 'balsams'. Under the name of 'Canada balsam', the resin is used by biologists to fix delicate specimens on microscope slides.

The timbers of silver firs resemble those of spruces, being white to very pale yellow throughout, easily worked, but only moderately strong.

97

They are used for the same purposes in the lumber and paper pulp industries. Silver fir timber is often mixed with spruce under the general description of 'whitewood'.

The hill ranges of the Jura, the Vosges, the Black Forest of Germany, the Italian Appennines and the Carpathians support vast forests of **European silver fir,** *Abies alba.* It is also a leading tree in the lower valleys of the Alps. It flourishes, better than most other conifers, in dry limestone soils. Individual specimens attain great sizes, up to 200 feet (61 m) tall and 30 feet (9·1 m) round.

Introduced to Britain around the beginning of the seventeenth century, silver fir once provided the country's largest recorded tree. A specimen at Inveraray in Argyll, Scotland, once scaled 180 feet (54·9 m) tall by 20 feet (6·1 m) round. Alas, this European species is now rarely planted in Britain, for a tiny aphid, *Adelges normannianae,*

cripples nearly every tree in its infancy. This insect, introduced accidentally from Asia, is found in Central Europe too, but under the different climate there it does no economic harm.

In place of the European species, British foresters now plant the American **giant fir,** *Abies grandis.* This originates on the Pacific seaboard from British Columbia to California. It is a beautiful tree with broad ranks of deep green needles, immune to the harmful aphid's attacks. In Oregon it may grow 300 feet (91·4 m) tall by 20 feet (6·1 m) round. In Britain it shows, in good sample plots, a faster rate of timber production than any other tree yet tried.

From the same Pacific region comes the **noble fir,** *A. procera,* a lovely conifer that bears its silvery, blue-green needles in dense masses, swept up towards the light and overlapping like the pile of some deep carpet. It forms a stout,

strongly tapering, upright trunk with smooth slate-grey bark. The very distinctive cones, often called 'feathercones', have a reflexed, feather-edged, and long-pointed bract below each scale. Scales and bracts together present a marvellously symmetric pattern of spirals. Noble fir is widely planted as an ornamental tree in many parts of Europe and its native America. In Denmark it has gained a firm place as the national Christmas tree. Its Red Indian name is *tuck-tuck*.

Another fine western conifer is the **white fir,** *A. concolor,* native to the mountains of California, Utah and Colorado. Adapted to a dry climate, it bears bluish-green needles two inches (51 mm) in length, in two loose ranks, and large purplish-green cones, up to five inches (127 mm) long.

The quaint little **Korean silver fir,** *A. koreana,* has become a favourite tree for garden planting because of its pretty flowers, which open in May. The males are red-brown and the females pink, red, or purple. The short cones are purple, with flecks of white resin and they are borne even by a very young tree—another attractive feature for the gardener. The short, blunt needles are dark green above and white below.

Left: Cone and foliage of white fir, Abies concolor, *from Colorado*

Below: Flowers of Korean silver fir, Abies koreana. *The females, left, are purplish-red cylinders. The males, which are on the right, form red-brown groups and shed yellow pollen*

Douglas Fir and Hemlocks

Douglas firs are among the tallest and stateliest trees of North America's western seaboard. They form great forests stretching along the coast from Alaska down to California and far inland up the slopes of the Rocky Mountains. This valuable economic resource is carefully husbanded by the forest authorities of Canada and the United States to ensure perpetual supplies of lumber for industry. Fortunately, these firs seed freely and natural regrowth soon fills the gaps cut in the virgin forest, though many forest owners find it more profitable to replant artificially.

The forester's name of 'Douglas fir' records an intrepid Scottish botanical explorer, David Douglas of Scone, Perthshire, who first sent seeds of this tree to Europe. In 1827, he achieved one of the first overland crossings of Canada, from Vancouver to Hudson Bay. The tree's scientific name, *Pseudotsuga menziesii,* recalls another Scottish botanist, Archibald Menzies, who collected specimens on Captain Vancouver's expedition in 1792.

Key characters of Douglas fir include a brown, torpedo-shaped bud, with several papery scales, rather like the bud of a beech tree. The needles, arranged in two loose ranks on side shoots, have no basal pegs and leave a round scar when pulled away. They are dark green and smell pleasantly when crushed, which explains the tree's Italian name of *abete odoroso,* the fragrant fir. The bark of young shoots is greyish-brown and smooth, except for oval resin blisters that exude clear, perfumed resin when broken. On old trunks the bark becomes immensely thick and rugged, exposing typical orange-brown patches below its purplish-grey exterior surface.

The male flowers form pink oval clusters of stamens, which shed abundant golden pollen in May. The female flowers which receive it are oval, bud-shaped and dark red at first, becoming green later. Below each soft scale there is a three-pointed bract, an unmistakable key feature. As these female flowers ripen into cones during the summer, both scales and bracts become brown and woody. In autumn the scales start to open and shed small, brown, oval-winged seeds, two from each scale. Seeds sprout readily next spring on damp earth. They bear a rosette of about six seed-leaves, then solitary needles around an upright shoot.

Douglas fir timber has a pale brown sapwood and a deep red-brown heartwood. In both these tissues there is always a well-developed summerwood zone to every annual ring, whether it be wide or narrow, and this ensures great strength. Because of the lumber's general resemblance to that of pine trees it is often marketed as 'British Columbian pine' or 'Oregon pine'. Available in long lengths and large diameters, it is widely used for building and engineering work, including docks and bridges. It is exported in quantity from North America to Europe and around the world. Big logs yield large, strong sheets of plywood, widely used for construction work as concrete shuttering, and in table tops and doors. Smaller logs and waste provide transmission poles, railway sleepers or ties, fencing, chipboard and paper pulp.

Douglas fir has been introduced as a timber producer to most countries of western Europe, including France, Italy and Germany. It has also been planted in New Zealand, Australia and South Africa. In the British Isles there are many productive plantations, and some exceptional specimen trees, though they prove susceptible to damage from high winds and thrive best in deep, well-watered valleys. Britain's tallest tree today is probably a Douglas fir in the Hermitage woods of Strath Braan, near Dunkeld in Perthshire, Scotland, which is 180 feet (54·9 m) high. The record for girth among Douglas firs in Britain is held by a tree at Dunkeld Cathedral nearby, 21 feet (6·4 m) round. The greatest volume, 20 cubic metres (706 cubic feet) of timber, has been measured in a felled New Forest specimen tree, only 110 years old.

Naturally these figures are easily exceeded in North America. In 1895, lumberjacks in the Capilano grove on Vancouver Island felled a Douglas fir which proved, after measurements on

the ground certified by the mayor and the sheriff, to have been the tallest tree ever known anywhere on earth! It scaled 417 feet (127 m), and was 50 feet (15·2 m) round.

Similar girths, and heights up to 300 feet (91·4 m) or even 350 feet (107 m) are still found occasionally in the State of Washington, but inevitably the largest, most accessible valley-floor trees have been felled. Ages of 1,140 years have been proved by ring-counts, and reliable estimates give 1,300 years for a giant growing on Vancouver Island.

Hemlock trees owe their curious name to the odour of their crushed foliage. This resembles that of the hemlock plant, *Conium maculatum,* a tall weed with large white flowers, a green stem with purple spots, and a poisonous sap, which grows along watersides in Europe. The trees were given this odd name, and also its French Canadian equivalent, *sapin ciguë,* by early colonists who encountered the eastern hemlock, *Tsuga canadensis,* growing freely in the forests of Quebec and New England where it is still a leading source of lumber. European foresters prefer to plant the western hemlock, *T. heterophylla,* native to America's Pacific seaboard, because it proves better fitted to their climate and grows a more shapely main stem. Its needles have parallel edges, while those of the eastern race taper.

The hemlocks are easily distinguished by the variable lengths of their small, blunt needles. There are actually three kinds; long, medium and short. These repeat in a spiral around the twigs. On side branches they lie, overall, in flat planes, with dark green upper surfaces, and paler undersides. Each needle arises from an oval 'cushion' on its twig. The soft, flexible leading

shoot of a hemlock always bends over and droops distinctly downwards. In this way it sheds snow and escapes storm damage. Nevertheless the tree grows steadily upwards, though no-one, as yet, fully understands the mechanism.

Hemlock's male flowers appear as clusters of crimson stamens amid the foliage in May, and scatter yellow, wind-borne pollen. The green, bud-shaped female flowers ripen rapidly after pollination. By October the whole crown becomes studded with small, bright brown egg-shaped cones. Their oval scales soon open and each releases two very small dark brown seeds, with pale brown, triangular, papery wings. When the seedling sprouts it always opens *three* seed-leaves, an unusual number. The normal varied needle pattern follows.

Hemlocks bear a thin, grey bark that soon breaks up into a shallow pattern of irregular rectangles. It is rich in tannin and in America it has been used on a large commercial scale for tanning hides to make leather. The timber of hemlock resembles spruce, but is somewhat stronger. Pale yellowish-brown in colour, with a darker heartwood, it is easily worked and widely used for house-building, joinery, box-making, chipboard and paper pulp.

Today hemlock is widely planted in European woods. It is a decorative tree that can stand shade and can be planted in small clearings, and it yields useful timber at a fast rate. There are also many beautiful old specimen trees with fine tapering crowns. One at Murthly Castle in Perthshire has reached 143 feet (43·6 m), and another at Scone Palace—the old home of David Douglas—measures 18 feet (5·5 m) round. Native trees in Oregon may stand for 500 years, reaching heights over 200 feet (61 m).

Cypresses and American Cedars

Italian cypress, *Cupressus sempervirens,* is the characteristic tree of the Mediterranean landscape. Slender, dark and stately, its upright columns blend perfectly with classical ruins or with Romanesque or Renaissance buildings, beneath a cloudless sky and a blazing sun. A close look at its densely packed foliage shows that the side branches follow the upright trend of the main stem, while every twig is completely clothed in small, scale-like leaves that clasp it, even hiding the buds. This foliage pattern is ideal for survival in a climate of hot, dry summers and cool, moist winters, for it exposes an effective leaf area to the sunlight, yet restricts water loss. Broader-crowned strains of Italian cypress are common in the wilds, and the Romans used their tough timber for building houses, temples and sea-going galleys. The columnar variety is preferred as a subject for landscape planting, although its timber is too knotty for building because of the many side branches.

Cypress bark is greyish-brown, thin and stringy. The timber has pale brown sapwood and deep brown inner heartwood. It is strong yet easily worked, and the heartwood is naturally durable. Because its fragrant oil repels insects, it is often used to make clothes chests.

In May, small green male flowers open near the twig tips and shed golden, wind-borne pollen. The female flowers are at first green and bud-shaped, but develop after fertilization into round, green cones, which turn brown as they ripen in autumn. Each woody cone has the shape that characterizes all 'true' cypresses, in the botanical sense. It is spherical, being built up of several scales that bear a flat head, usually with a central knob, on a slender stalk. Each scale produces, beneath its sheltering surface, about 20 small seeds. Each seed bears, along its sides, two narrow papery wings. Seeds are shed through the winter, and are dispersed by the wind.

When the seeds sprout in spring they open two, three or four seed-leaves. 'Juvenile' foliage follows, made up of pointed slender needles, standing clear of the little stem. In the tree's second year of life the close-ranked, stem-clasping 'adult' needles first appear.

Spanish missionaries who travelled from Mexico north to California found, near Monterey, a grove of rugged native cypress trees. This race, now known as the **Monterey cypress,** *Cupressus macrocarpa,* resembles the Italian cypress closely, but has larger and more knobbly cones.

Under the harsh environment of the exposed Pacific coast, Monterey cypress grows very slowly. Though the storm-swept veterans look highly picturesque, with ancient gnarled stems and flat-topped crowns, few have topped 60 feet (18·3 m). When introduced to kindlier surroundings this cypress grows exceptionally fast, and it has therefore been planted for timber in New Zealand, Australia, South and East Africa, and South America. Its tolerance of salt-laden gales makes it a valuable tree for coastal shelter-belts and it has been widely planted beside gardens along many European coastlines. In the British Isles it proves fully hardy only near the warm Gulf Stream, notably in Cornwall, western Wales and Ireland. The tallest tree measured, at Tregothnan near Truro in Cornwall, is 120 feet (36·6 m) high, or twice the height of Californian natives. Others exceed 30 feet (9·1 m) in girth. Farther north, east, or inland, Monterey cypresses are apt to die suddenly after prolonged spells of hard frost.

Arizona cypress, *Cupressus arizonica,* is a smaller tree adapted to life under desert conditions. It grows on the high, arid mountains of Arizona, Utah and northern Mexico. It is also very resistant to cold. Its grey-green needles hug the twigs tightly and the knobbly cones, an inch (25 mm) across, are a shiny greenish-brown, with a waxy, silvery-grey bloom. This neat evergreen has been widely planted in both European and American parks and gardens.

Another attractive ornamental tree from America's south-west is the **incense cedar,** *Calocedrus decurrens.* This is usually known on sight from its erect, columnar habit, with side branches following the upward trend of the trunk. Its deep

Above: Silvery foliage and cones of Arizona cypress,
Cupressus arizonica. *Close-ranked needles, pressed against
the twigs, and large round cones are typical of this genus*

Opposite page: An impressive grove of Italian cypresses

*Left: Fragrant incense cedar, native to California, forms a
dramatic, dark, upright column*

green foliage forms flat fronds and, if you crush
it, gives forth the strong, pleasing, incense-like
fragrance that explains the tree's name. Incense
cedar has a thin, fibrous, pinkish-brown bark.
Its sapwood is pale yellow and its heartwood pale
pinkish-brown. Since it can be worked very
smoothly it is used to make good pencils.
Specimen trees of incense cedar can be found,
striking their effective note, in many European
and American ornamental gardens.

Lawson cypress, *Chamacyparis lawsoniana*, also
called Port Orford cedar, has become one of the
most widely planted evergreens for decoration
and hedging in all temperate lands. Its foliage is
also widely used by florists everywhere. It is
named after Peter Lawson, an Edinburgh nurseryman and the promoter of an exploration by the
Scottish botanist Andrew Murray who found this
cypress growing beside the Sacramento River
in 1854.

Left: Fern-like foliage of Lawson cypress, Chamaecyparis lawsoniana, *with clusters of crimson male flowers and minute, blue female flowers at twig tips*

In its native forests, which extend from Oregon south to California, this cypress ranks as a minor tree, found in clearings or along stream banks among giant spruces and hemlocks. Its moderate rate of growth, however, proves an advantage in gardens or small urban spaces. It stands shade, holds its foliage low down and keeps an even green outer surface without clipping. Many varieties show different foliage colours—golden, blue, or variegated with silver, and there are dwarf, columnar, and low spreading strains. These are readily propagated by striking cuttings.

Despite these variations, Lawson cypress is easily identified by its very flat sprays of foliage, which resemble the fronds of a fern. The leaves, instead of being grouped evenly round squarish twigs, as in Monterey cypress, form a flat plane, dark green above and paler below. They completely hide the buds, which are so minute that they cannot even be felt through the little leaves that surround them. When crushed the foliage gives off a characteristically sharp, sour odour.

Lawson cypress bears, in May, minute flowers at the tips of its sprays. The male flowers form pretty pink clusters of stamens that shed fine yellow pollen. Female flowers are bluish-green, and look like open buds made up of small triangular scales. The cones mature the following autumn, changing from green to reddish-brown. They are about the size of a pea, and have about a dozen flat-headed scales, each carrying a small central prickle. As the scales open, each releases about five tiny seeds, small brown oval grains with a broad, thin papery wing down each side. When they sprout, each seed opens just two oval seed-leaves. Solitary, sharply pointed 'juvenile' leaves follow, and in its first year the seedling looks like a little juniper bush. The characteristically flat 'adult' spray of foliage, with needles hiding twig and buds, appears in the second year.

The timber of Lawson cypress has a pale yellow sapwood and a pale brown, naturally durable heartwood. It is strong and easily worked, and is employed in western North America for building, joinery, fencing and furniture. It holds a sharply smelling oil, which is believed to repel insects; hence it is used for clothes chests. In Europe this handsome cypress is only planted for ornament, because its stem is very apt to fork, resulting in logs of low value. The fibrous bark on mature trunks is a shining brown, and is vertically ridged.

Leyland cypress, *Cupressocyparis leylandii*, is a remarkable hybrid tree. Its male parent is the Alaska cedar, *Chamaecyparis nootkatensis*, a

northern species which resembles a Lawson cypress but has larger pointed knobs to its cone scales, and its female parent is the Monterey cypress. These two trees first interbred around 1888 on the Leighton Hall estate near Welshpool, mid-Wales, owned by a Mr Leyland. This hybrid, which is easily increased by cuttings, grows very fast and is often planted in gardens when an evergreen screen is needed quickly. It can grow up to 100 feet (30·5 m) tall.

The **American cedars** of the genus *Thuja* have sprays of fern-like foliage very like the Lawson cypress. If, however, you take a spray between your fingers, you can feel definite swellings caused by the hidden buds. The cones differ in being long and slender, with about ten pale brown and incurved scales joined only at the base. The tiny brown seeds have a long oval outline, with slender, thin wings down each side. Seedlings start life with two seed-leaves, then 'juvenile' foliage of free, slender, sharply pointed needles appears, followed by the 'adult' fronds.

These cedars' flowers, which open in April, are very small and rarely attract attention. The male ones, clustered at twig tips, are crimson until they spread their yellow pollen. The female ones have open groups of green scales, tipped with black, and are also located at the twig tips.

The bark of American cedars is thin, reddish-brown, and stringy. Their timber has a pale yellow, almost white sapwood and a distinct red-brown heartwood that has remarkable natural durability. The wood as a whole is exceptionally light and strong. It has been widely used in North America since colonial days for traditional wooden roofing shingles, and field boundaries such as 'split-cedar' and 'snake' fences. It is a good building timber easily split by a pioneer's

Above: This columnar form of eastern white cedar, from New England, gives striking landscape effects. It is Thuja occidentalis *variety* pyramidalis

Right: Fronds of western red cedar, bearing oval cones with long, loose scales

axe to yield thin boards without the labour of sawing. It makes ideal ladder poles, and is the best material for garden frames, greenhouses, and window framing.

Northern white cedar, *Thuja occidentalis,* is common throughout eastern Canada and New England, especially on marshlands, but it only makes a small tree, up to 50 feet (15·2 m) high.

In contrast, the **western red cedar,** *Thuja plicata,* native to British Columbia and Washington, grows into an enormous tree with a huge buttressed base, up to 200 feet (61 m) tall and 50 feet (15·2 m) round. In the past the Haida Indians used its wood for building their houses. They hollowed out large trunks to make sea-going war canoes, and set up others as carved and painted totem poles. Today, western red cedar is the mainstay of a big timber trade, for both home use and world-wide export.

Western red cedar has proved thoroughly at home in Britain, where it was introduced in 1853, and throughout most of western Europe. It is planted as hedges, as an ornamental tree, as a source of decorative foliage, and increasingly for timber. It yields high volumes of strong, useful wood, tolerates chalk and limestone soils that discourage other conifers, and proves fully hardy even in Scotland.

Above: Western red cedar, found on America's Pacific coast, has a typical buttressed base with stringy bark

Left: A shapely young specimen tree of western red cedar

Sequoias and their allies

California is the homeland of two amazing conifers, one the world's tallest living tree and the other the world's largest. They are closely related, and share, in one form or another the name 'sequoia'. This commemorates the famous Indian chief Sequoyah, the son of a Cherokee princess by a German father, who lived far away in Tennessee in the eighteenth century, and invented an alphabet for his people.

First to be discovered was the **coast redwood**, *Sequoia sempervirens*, sighted by the Spaniard Don Gaspar da Pabola, when he explored the hinterland of San Francisco Bay in 1769. Here he found, growing in the fog belt that fringes the Pacific Ocean, dense groves of magnificent dark-foliaged evergreens that soared higher than any other trees known. Their straight, slowly tapering trunks had immensely thick, very fibrous, soft, rust-red bark, deeply fissured between ribs that met at intervals like Gothic arches. Many rose for 100 feet (30·5 m) without a side branch.

Leaves plucked from saplings proved remarkably like those of a common yew. They grew in two ranks of flat needles, dark green above and paler below. A distinguishing feature, handy for every botanist, is that on the redwood the needles of each year's shoot growth vary in length, being shorter towards the tip and longer nearer the base. This variation is very even and gives the frond a peculiarly boat-shaped outline. Another difference is that there are always short scales present at the base of the redwood's leaf frond, and when it eventually fades, after several years of life, it falls in one piece, not as separate needles as do the fronds of the yew. Upright shoots bear solitary needles, set spirally round the stem.

When redwoods were felled they proved to hold, below their thick bark, a thin zone of pale yellow sapwood. Below this lay their immensely thick heartwood, reddish brown in colour, naturally durable, strong and easily worked. This soon became a staple timber for Californian settlers, and eventually the mainstay of a major sawmilling industry. Fortunately regrowth after felling is rapid. Seedlings spring up in clearings, and the stumps of felled trees send up vigorous coppice shoots or sprouts, an unusual feature for a conifer.

The time needed to grow a giant redwood is measured by hundreds and even thousands of years. The Californians realized, just in time, that their unique veterans were in peril from the lumberman's axe, and the finest were preserved in national parks. The official height record is 367 feet (112 m) for a tree on the Dyerville Flats. Another contender, in a deep valley nearby is said, however, to scale 384 feet (117 m). The stoutest, nicknamed 'General Custer', is 66 feet (20·1 m) round, holds over 1,200 cubic metres (42,380 cubic feet) of timber, weighing 1,200 tons, and has an estimated age of 2,000 years. Actual ring counts on felled redwoods run up to 2,200 years.

These terrific trees arise from tiny seeds. In spring certain twigs develop curious foliage, made up of short, scaly needles set all round the twig tips. Some of these bear male flowers, little oval groups of green anthers that shed yellow, wind-borne pollen; others bear female flowers, small oval structures composed of green, spine-tipped fertile scales. After fertilization these flowers ripen during the following summer. They become brown, oval, woody cones, about half an inch (13 mm) across, which persist on twigs for many years. There are about 20 cone scales, each with a central stalk, a broad outer face and a little prickle. About six seeds develop beneath each scale. They are barely a sixteenth of an inch (1·6 mm) long, brown and oval, and fringed with two thin, united, papery wings that aid their dispersal by wind.

The minute seedling, quite unlike the parent tree, starts life with two oblong seed-leaves, and then bears solitary needles set spirally round its upright shoot. Typical side fronds first appear a full year later.

The coast redwood was introduced to Russia in about 1840 and during the ensuing 20 years specimens were planted on numerous country estates throughout western Europe. Nowhere,

Above: Giant sequoias standing in a natural grove, now a national park in California. The world's largest trees, they can exceed 300 feet (91·4 m) in height, and 3,000 years in age

Right: Cone and leaves of coast redwood. Some needles follow the twigs, others form boat-shaped fronds

Left: A fine specimen of coast redwood in Melbury, Dorset, southern England

however, does it find conditions quite so congenial as in its native California.

In the British Isles the record for height among the redwoods is held by a tree 136 feet (41·5 m) tall at Taymouth Castle in Perthshire, Scotland, and that for girth is 23 feet (7 m) round, held by a tree at Inistioge, County Kilkenny, Ireland; both trees are about 120 years old. The Royal Forestry Society owns a small but impressive plantation at Leighton Hall, near Welshpool in mid-Wales.

The marvellous **giant sequoia,** *Sequoiadendron giganteum*, has survived as a native tree in only a few valleys in the Californian mountains. There it remained unknown, save to Indian hunters, until an explorer named John Bidwell stumbled into a grove near the source of the Sacramento River in the Sierra Nevada mountains in 1841. His reports were at first discredited, but by 1853 collectors were sending seed to the eastern States and also to Europe. There are now known to be about 70 isolated groves, mostly in deep valleys at altitudes of 5,000 to 8,000 feet (1,524 m to 2,438 m). Here, in an arid climate of hot summers and cold, snowy winters, they have persisted for countless thousands of years, escaping destruction during the ice ages. The rarity of this tree was soon appreciated. Nearly all these woods have long been preserved as national parks and no timber trade has developed. In its technical properties the slow-grown Californian timber resembles that of redwood, but faster growth in Europe yields light, weak, material.

The bark of the giant sequoia differs from that of the coast redwood in being pale grey, but it is equally thick, soft and fibrous, with similar interlaced ribs and fissures. You can strike either tree a hard blow with your fist and still leave your knuckles unharmed. The foliage is quite different from the redwood foliage. Giant sequoia has an overlapping armour of tough, pointed pale green needles, which clothe the twigs and hide the buds. They project evenly all round every twig. After a life of several years they fade and fall away, in short, withered branchlets.

Male and female flowers of the giant sequoia resemble those of the coast redwood, betraying their close botanical relationship. Its cones, however, are larger, around two inches (51 mm) across, and they take two years to ripen fully, becoming woody and reddish-brown. The seeds have broader wings than those of coast redwood. Seedlings bear from three to five narrow seed leaves, followed by typical needles.

The largest, though not the tallest, tree standing today is the giant sequoia named 'General Grant'. This measures 267 feet (81·4 m) tall by 80 feet (24·4 m) round, and has a volume of 2,000 cubic metres (70,632 cubic feet) of timber, weighing about 2,000 tons. With the addition of branches, foliage and roots, the total weight of this giant is probably 2,500 tons: all the outcome of continuous growth from a single tiny seed, weighing only 0·5 mg. The age of the 'General Grant' tree is estimated at 3,500 years, based on ring counts on comparable felled stems. The tallest known giant sequoia scales 320 feet (97·5 m), and the greatest accepted age is 4,000 years.

Seeds of the giant sequoia were sent to Europe in 1853, and it quickly became popular, both because of its reputation and for the beauty of the pale green colouring and conical outlines of young specimens. It has proved hardy and adaptable, and can be found on numerous private estates and in large public gardens. In Britain it was called 'Wellingtonia' in honour of the great soldier and statesman the Duke of Wellington, who had died just before it was discovered, and this name remains in popular use, although only in the British Isles.

Under cultivation amid open surroundings the giant sequoia maintains its shapely conical outline, with green branches down to ground level, to a surprising size and age. Britain's tallest, at Endsleigh near Tavistock in Devon, is 165 feet

Left: Cones and foliage of giant sequoia, with yellow male flowers at the twig tips. All the needles follow, and clasp, the twigs

(50·3 m) high, while the stoutest, at Crichel House in Dorset, is 30 feet (9·1 m) round. With centuries of life ahead, such giants may eventually challenge those of California, though records are more likely to be broken under the warmer climate of Italy. Giant sequoia has long been a popular ornamental tree in the eastern United States, and it also thrives in South Africa and Australia.

Swamp cypress, *Taxodium distichum*, originates in the marshlands bordering creeks, lakes and rivers in Florida and neighbouring states of the south-eastern United States where it forms extensive forests. It is valued for the lumber which is harvested by winching felled logs on to floating barges. Its branches are often festooned by a hanging epiphytic plant called 'Spanish moss', not a true moss but a higher plant named *Tillandsia usneoides*.

Swamp cypress shows curious adaptations to life in the Everglades and similar swamps which, though hot and steaming in summer, become cold in winter. In autumn its lovely, feathery green foliage turns bright orange-brown, and then falls. Its leafless appearance in winter explains its apt American name of 'bald cypress'. The base of its trunk is always strongly buttressed, a device to spread its weight and ensure support on soft, swampy soil. Its roots send up strange, knobbly,

Right: A shapely giant sequoia, or 'Wellingtonia', in Alice Holt Forest, Hampshire, England

grey 'knees', which rise a few inches above ground level. These are called 'pneumatophores', (literally 'air carriers') and their function is to carry oxygen down to the roots below the water. All roots must breathe; near moving water they gain oxygen dissolved in the water itself, but in stagnant bogs they need the extra supply carried by the open-textured 'knee' roots.

This remarkable tree bears a thin, rust-red bark that breaks away slowly in fibrous threads. Its sapwood is pale yellow, while its inner heartwood is red-brown, strong, stable, and naturally durable. It is used in the southern States for high-grade building work, particularly window frames and greenhouse construction, since it resists the weather. The leaves, which spring from small, scaly buds, form pretty fronds that fall in one piece when the foliage withers in autumn. The male flowers of swamp cypress develop in slender, long-stalked catkins, which open in spring. They are purple in general colour, and each flower is a cluster of anthers that shed yellow, wind-borne pollen.

Female flowers resemble those of coast redwood. The cones are round, brown and woody, with angular scales, and they measure $\frac{1}{2}$ inch (13 mm) across. Below each scale several seeds ripen, each a hard triangular grain with only a

vestige of a wing. They are spread by floating on water and sprout on mud. Each seedling has six slender seed-leaves, then solitary, thin, juvenile needles until the adult fronds appear.

Introduced to Europe in 1840, swamp cypress has been planted in many waterside gardens for its attractive foliage. It grows 117 feet (35·7 m) tall in Britain and 150 feet (45·7 m) in its native America. Records for girth are 18 feet (5·5 m) in Britain, and over 37 feet (11·3 m) in the southern United States.

The world's stoutest tree is probably a **Montezuma cypress,** *Taxodium mucronatum,* growing at Santa Maria del Tule, Oaxaca, Mexico. This close relative of the swamp cypress measures 115 feet (35 m) round, is 140 feet (42·7 m) tall, and has an estimated age of 3,500 years.

The **dawn redwood,** *Metasequoia glyptostroboides,* is a rare deciduous tree, closely resembling a swamp cypress, that survives only in the hidden, landlocked Shui-sa-pa Valley, 50 miles (80 km) south of the town of Wan-hsien in Szechwan, southern China. There it was discovered, as recently as 1941, by a Chinese forester named Tsang Wang, who had been sent in search of wartime timber supplies. It grows by streams, and forms an oddly indented, irregular trunk, with pinkish-brown bark, up to 100 feet (30·5 m) high

and seven feet (2·1 m) round. It has a buff-coloured sapwood and an orange or purplish-red heartwood. Dawn redwood is sometimes called the 'living fossil', because it was well known from fossilized remains before the surviving trees were discovered.

The dawn redwood's thin red-brown twigs are unique, among all trees, in bearing buds *below* leaves, instead of above them. The green branchlets, bearing flat green needles, arise in opposite pairs, whereas those of swamp cypress arise alternately. In autumn the foliage blazes in shades of bright orange before falling. The quaint, round cones develop on long stalks, hanging downwards. Seed was exported from China to the Arnold Arboretum at Boston, Massachusetts, in 1948, and the resulting plants were distributed to Kew Gardens near London, and to other leading gardens. It was then found that this pretty conifer is easily increased by cuttings, and it is now widely planted in parks and gardens.

The **Japanese cedar** or sugi, *Cryptomeria japonica*, forms large forests, valued for timber, on the mountains of southern Japan. Its pale green foliage is made up of slender, sharply pointed needles that hide the twigs because of the size and density of their bases, although their tips bend forwards and stand clear of the twig. The sturdy trunk, which can reach 150 feet (45·7 m) in height, and 25 feet (7·6 m) round in Japan, is clad in thin, red-brown, fibrous bark. The timber within has a pale yellow sapwood and a red-brown heartwood that is strong, naturally durable and easily worked.

Male flowers arise in leaf axils, as clusters of green stamens shedding yellow pollen. Female flowers, which resemble minute rosettes of green or purplish leaves, ripen in one summer to pretty cones with frilly scales. Below these scales numerous small, hard, brown, wingless seeds develop. Seedlings bear three seed-leaves, followed by soft needles and then by the typical hard, pointed kind.

The Japanese cedar is valued as an ornamental tree in Japan, where it has been widely planted in impressive long avenues and in temple gardens. It was introduced to the western world in 1842, but proves fully at home only in southern Europe, the southern United States and countries with similar climates. Mountain-top Japanese cedars grow slowly, but survive to ages approaching 4,000 years! In the warmer districts of the British Isles specimen trees have reached heights of 120 feet (36·6 m) and girths of 14 feet (4·3 m) after 100 years of growth.

A quaint variety of this handsome tree, named *elegans*, is widely planted in gardens and public parks. It retains soft, loose, 'juvenile' needles all through life. In autumn this attractive foliage changes from bluish-green to bronze shades, but it resumes its true colours next spring.

This *elegans* variety, despite its name, rarely forms an elegant, symmetrical tree. Instead it builds up a rather floppy, shapeless bush. This form attracts landscape architects when they wish to use a shapeless mass to fill or break up awkward symmetrical surfaces. Hence, this odd tree, which was brought to Britain and North America from Japanese gardens in 1861, has become popular for town planting schemes.

Yew and Juniper

Yew trees spread their dark, evergreen foliage, borne on low, ribbed, red-brown trunks, over hillsides throughout most of Europe and North America, and, in limited areas, on certain Asiatic mountain ranges. In Europe yews have long been associated with Christian churchyards, partly as symbols of eternal life, but, more practically, it seems probable that they served as shelter and meeting places for early congregations who had not yet built a church. Churchyard yews in Britain reach great size and age through long protection on hallowed ground: the greatest umbrage, or spread of branches, is 80 feet (24·4 m) across and is found at Tandridge in Surrey, on a yew of 35 feet (10·7 m) girth. Llanerfyl church in Montgomeryshire, Wales, has a yew with a trunk 40 feet (12·2 m) round, and 56½ feet (17·2 m) was once measured round the bole or trunk, now decrepit, of the churchyard yew at Fortingall, Perthshire, Scotland. From known rates of outward growth such trees must be well over 1,000 years old, possibly 1,500 years in the case of the Fortingall specimen, which may be the oldest living tree in Europe.

Yew leaves, or needles, are set in two ranks along thin twigs. They are slender, dark and glossy green above, pale green below. On emerging on young spring shoots from small buds, they are soft and pale throughout. They soon become tough, and each endures for about three years before fading and falling. Cattle, sheep and horses browse odd sprays of living yew foliage without suffering harm, but cut foliage becomes a deadly poison during the process of withering, both to farm livestock and to man.

Yew trees are either male or female. In February, the male trees bear pretty clusters of creamy yellow flowers, each holding a group of stamens that scatter wind-borne pollen. Flowers on female trees are, at this time, no more than green leafy buds with small stigmas to catch pollen. By October they have ripened to conspicuous pinkish-red berries, threading the dark foliage with colour. On each green base stands the fleshy, round, pink pulp or aril, which attracts the birds that spread the seeds. It has a sweet, sickly taste, but is not poisonous. Within it stands a single seed, greenish-black, hard and very poisonous to man. Birds however can swallow it whole and void it unharmed. When the seeds sprout, 18 months after ripening, they put forth two oblong, green, soft and deciduous seed-leaves. Normal evergreen foliage follows.

Yew bark, which is poisonous, is a dull, rusty brown and flakes away in patches. The trunks are too short and irregular for most timber uses, though valuable for crafts. Their outer sapwood zone is very thin, white and not naturally durable. The strong heartwood within is a lovely, rich red-brown shade with darker summerwood bands, and has exceptional durability. Its prime use is in archery bows, which are narrow staves cleft by hand from selected stems. Other uses of yew are in decorative furniture, sculpture, turned bowls, trays and trinkets. Rough logs make lasting fence posts, or good firewood.

The common yew of Europe is *Taxus baccata*. North America has three native kinds: the Canadian yew, *T. canadensis*, in the east, which is rarely more than a shrub, the western yew, *T. brevifolia*, and the Florida yew, *T. floridana*. In

Left: This ancient, spreading yew stands like a sentinel, high on a chalk down in southern England

Right: On a male yew, clusters of flowers open in early spring on the undersides of leafy twigs

Left: Foliage and berries of a female yew tree. The needles are dark green above and pale green below. Each rose-red berry holds one olive-green seed, which ripens in autumn

1780, an Irish farmer named Willis found, on the estate of the Earl of Enniskillen in County Fermanagh, a curious yew that grew straight upwards, with small side branches, like a Lombardy poplar. This 'Irish yew' has been widely propagated by grafting, and is now grown in gardens in all temperate lands. There are attractive golden-leaved varieties—some upright, others with normal growth habit. The tallest recorded yews, 90 feet (27·4 m) high, grow in the Close Walks, Midhurst, Sussex.

Yews cast denser shade than any other tree; the floor of a yew wood is bare because there is insufficient light for any green plants. But yew's own foliage endures deep shade and its leaves

crowd close together. It is excellent for close-clipped evergreen hedges and ideal for topiary—the gardener's art of training and clipping trees into fanciful shapes, such as castles, human figures, or peacocks.

Common juniper, *Juniperus communis,* is unique in showing the same characteristics all round the globe—across America, Europe and Asia. It has a circumpolar distribution, and thrives abundantly on peat or acid, sandy soils in the cold northern zone between the frozen tundra and the coniferous forests. It is common, too, on high mountain ranges farther south, including the Scottish Highlands, the Pyrenees, the Alps and Apennines and the American Appalachians and Rockies. Usually it is a low, shapeless bush, though upright forms occur locally in Sweden and Italy, and are cultivated in gardens. Here and there, juniper grows wild on limestone ranges including chalk downs in southern England, which are, of course, alkaline.

The foliage, berries, bark and even timber of juniper are fragrant with the resinous scent of 'oil of juniper'. Gin drinkers quickly recognize this, because this oil, distilled commercially from wood or berries, is used to flavour their pure grain spirit. Lovers of Polish juniper-smoked hams or Austrian juniper-smoked cheeses appreciate the piquant character of foods cured with the smoke of leaves and branchwood. Juniper branches burn brightly with a pleasing odour and are used in northern and montane lands for kindling fires. The pinkish-brown wood is only large enough for oddments like ornaments or

Left: Spiky foliage of juniper, with the soft, fragrant berries. The berries take two years to mature

Above: A shrubby juniper on an acid-soil hillside in the English Lake District. Juniper also thrives on alkaline chalk soils

short tool handles, though it is strong and supple.

Juniper is known at once by its scent and by its spiky foliage which is like that of a gorse bush. Silvery, bluish-green, spiky needles, grouped in threes, stick out at all angles, hiding the thin twigs. Each lasts about five years, and its glossy, tough surface resists water loss during cold or dry conditions. Buds are minute. The stem bark is grey and fibrous and flakes away slowly.

Clusters of small yellow male flowers, which shed wind-borne pollen, open in March amid the needles. Female flowers open at the same time, appearing close by in smaller groups as green

bud-shaped structures. Following pollination, they swell to become green, fleshy globes, with blunt angular spikes, which are actually modified seed-bearing scales. Botanically, juniper is a conifer, although it bears berries. By October of the following year these pea-sized berries are fully ripe, bluish-black and succulent. Throughout the winter they attract birds, especially grouse and thrushes, who spread the seeds. There are from one to five seeds in each berry and when they sprout, 18 months later, they bear two long, narrow, deciduous seed-leaves before the usual evergreen needles develop.

Monkey Puzzle, Maidenhair Tree and Umbrella Pine

The bizarre **monkey puzzle tree** or Chile pine, *Araucaria araucana*, is native to the high ranges of the southern Andes, on the borders of Argentina and Chile. No monkeys haunt these chilly, snow-swept slopes, so the tree was not given its odd common name until 1834, when an eminent lawyer, Charles Austin, after handling a specimen tree in Cornwall declared that it would be 'a puzzle for a monkey to climb'. Its scientific names commemorate the fierce Araucanian Indians who for long maintained their independence of the Spanish settlers. Each autumn they visited groves of monkey puzzle trees to collect the large nutritious seeds, which they stored as a winter food reserve. Eventually, some seeds were served as a dessert at a banquet given by the Spaniards in Valparaiso, in 1795, to Captain Vancouver's visiting British ship the *Discovery*. Archibald Menzies, the ship's scientist, took some seeds back to England and so introduced this curious tree to Europe.

Monkey puzzle belongs to a peculiar family of conifers, the Araucariaceae, found wild mainly in the Southern Hemisphere. Its dark green, glossy needles are broad, thick, and triangular in shape. They stand in spirals, overlapping and hiding both stems and buds. They live for up to 15 years before they fade and fall. Their basal scars persist on the stems for another ten years or so, but eventually only traces remain on otherwise smooth, dark green bark. At the base of the tree the bark becomes wrinkled, and resembles an elephant's foot.

Each spring the monkey puzzle extends its crown by sending up a stout leading shoot and putting out four or five side branches. There are no intermediate twigs, and the characteristic geometrical branching pattern suggests that this odd tree was designed by an unimaginative engineer working for a hidebound government department! Eventually, however, some branches do droop gracefully. On its native Andes, monkey puzzle attains heights of 150 feet (45·7 m), with girths up to 15 feet (4·6 m). In the British Isles it has grown to 87 feet (26·5 m) in height, with a girth of 12 feet (3·6 m).

Male and female flowers appear on separate trees as a rule, but they may occasionally appear on the same one. The male flowers, which open in May, are large, conspicuous, cylindrical

Left: Monkey puzzle builds up a rounded crown, although its sweeping boughs follow an angular branching pattern

Right: Shoot and cone of monkey puzzle. The triangular leaves, ranked in neat spirals, can remain on the tree for as long as ten years

clusters of yellow pollen-bearing scales, which persist on the tree for some years. Female flowers are large, oval structures, built up of many oval, green scales interspersed with slender green bracts. They expand during the following summer, and then resemble small, green pineapples. Two years after their first appearance they mature, turn yellowish-brown, and slowly break up. From below each scale there falls a single, large brown seed. This is triangular to oval in shape, and holds a white nutritious kernel, which becomes tasty when cooked. It bears a rudimentary wing, too small for wind dispersal, and the seed is spread in the wilds by birds and other animals.

The seedling of monkey puzzle differs from nearly all other conifers in retaining its seed-leaves, which are two in number, within its husk when it sprouts. Typical stout triangular needles appear from the outset on the upright shoot.

Monkey puzzle timber is a useful softwood, with a cream-coloured sapwood zone and a pale-brown heartwood having a characteristic pink tinge. Tiny knots within it, set spirally, are traces of the veins that ran to former leaves. In South America the wood is extensively used for building, fencing and packaging. The similar timber of a related tree, the more abundant Parana pine, *A. brasiliana*, found in Brazil, is regularly exported to Europe and North America as a reliable, easily worked material for joinery, interior finish, and household furniture making. Another member of this quaint group is the Norfolk Island pine, *A. excelsa*, a tender tropical tree grown in greenhouses to make an exotic display in public halls on ceremonial occasions.

Maidenhair tree, *Gingko biloba*, draws its name from the resemblance of its foliage to the fronds of the maidenhair fern, *Adiantum capillus-veneris*. Its leaves are unlike those of any other tree alive, either broadleaved or conifer. Each is fan-shaped, with a short stalk and numerous veins that spread out from the base. The end is flat or rounded, with a shallow central notch that explains the term *biloba*, meaning two-lobed. Most leaves arise in bunches from woody, ridged, short shoots, that project from the main twigs. Leaves that grow near twig tips are solitary. All the pale green leaves open in spring and turn a lovely golden colour before they fall in autumn.

Maidenhair tree is in fact a remarkable survivor of a large group of woody plants that flourished in the Carboniferous era, 250 million years ago. Their fossils are often found by miners in the world's coal seams. The other trees died out long ago. Maidenhair tree itself survives as a wild tree only in a few groves of south-west China, though it has been cultivated for centuries, under the

Above: Japanese umbrella pine Sciadopitys verticillata, bears odd double needles radiating like the ribs of a parasol. Its oval cones have rounded, fan-shaped scales

names of *pa-kwo* and *yin-kuo* (hence gingko), in temple gardens throughout China and Japan. Today it is grown in parks and large gardens in all temperate countries. In some American districts it is often planted as a street tree.

Every maidenhair tree is either male or female. The males bear clusters of catkin-like flowers that spring, in May, from their side shoots. Each individual catkin consists of many flowers ranged along a long stalk. They shed yellow, wind-borne pollen and then wither. The female flowers arise, usually in pairs, as acorn-shaped structures at the tips of the long, green stalks which spring from the short shoots of female trees. In autumn they ripen to yellow-skinned, plum-shaped fruits, with a soft, strongly smelling, edible yellow pulp and a single hard stone or seed. Birds scatter these seeds, which sprout next spring, just like an acorn. Their seed-leaves, two in number, remain within the husk. The first true leaves that follow are scale-like and rudimentary. Normal lobed leaves develop later.

The bark of maidenhair tree is grey and smooth in youth, but becomes thick and furrowed later. The pale yellow-brown timber below is fairly

Top left: The graceful maidenhair tree develops lovely golden tints before its leaves fall in autumn. These unique leaves, shown bottom left, have fan-shaped blades with radiating veins, and arise on long stalks from curious, short shoots

strong and easily worked, but too scarce for commercial marketing. Under cultivation in Europe the maidenhair tree can gain a height of 120 feet (36·6 m), and a girth of 15 feet (4·6 m). The finest specimen trees stand in Italy. There is a remarkably beautiful old tree in the Royal Botanic Gardens at Kew in Surrey which was planted in 1796 and is still flourishing.

Umbrella pine, *Sciadopitys verticillata*, grows its quaint foliage in a unique way. Its dark green needles are fused into pairs, with deep grooves along the join. They stand out from the scaly twigs like the ribs of an umbrella, which explains its name. At branch tips this odd tree bears clusters of oval, yellow, male flowers or small, green, conical female ones. The latter ripen into egg-shaped cones with broad, rounded scales, each concealing five or six winged seeds. Umbrella pine grows wild in the forests of Hondo, Japan, forming a slender, thin-barked tree, up to 120 feet (36·6 m) high. Its timber has a yellow sapwood with a browner heart, and is used in boat-building. In Europe and America the umbrella pine grows slowly and is cultivated solely as a bizarre ornamental tree.

Selected reading list

Bean, W.J. *Trees and Shrubs Hardy in the British Isles*, John Murray, London, 8th edn. 1970

Boom, B.K. and Kleijn, H. *The glory of the tree*, Harrap, London 1966

Brockman, C.F. *Trees of North America*, Golden Press, New York 1968

Colvin, B. and Tyrwhitt, J. *Trees for Town and Country*, Lund Humphries, London, 3rd edn. 1961

Dallimore, W., Jackson, A.B. and Harrison, S.G. *A Handbook of Coniferae and Ginkgoaceae*, Edward Arnold, London, 4th edn. 1966

Edlin, H.L. *Guide to Tree Planting and Cultivation*, Collins, London 1970

Edlin, H.L. *Trees, Woods and Man*, Collins, London, 3rd edn. 1970

Edlin H.L. *Wayside and Woodland Trees*, Frederick Warne, London and New York 1964

Edlin, H.L. *What Wood is That?* Thames and Hudson, London 1969

Edlin, H.L. and Nimmo, M. *Treasury of Trees*, Countrygoer Books, Manchester 1956

Everett, T.H. *Living Trees of the World*, Thames and Hudson, London 1969

Hadfield, M. *British Trees*, Dent, London 1957

Hart, C.E. *Practical Forestry for the Agent and Surveyor*, Estates Gazette, London 1967

Hart, C.E. and Raymond, C. *British Trees in Colour*, Michael Joseph, London 1973

Hosie, R.C. *Native Trees of Canada*, Canadian Department of Forestry and Rural Development, Queen's Printer for Canada, Ottawa, 7th edn. 1969

Johnson, H. *The International Book of Trees*, Mitchell Beazley, London 1973, Simon and Schuster, New York 1973

Mitchell, A.F. *Conifers in the British Isles*, Forestry Commission Booklet 33, Her Majesty's Stationery Office, London 1972

Ovington, J.D. *Woodlands*, English Universities Press, London 1965

U.S. Department of Agriculture. *Woody-Plant Seed Manual*, prepared by the Forest Service, Miscellaneous Publication No. 654, U.S. Government Printing Office, Washington, 1948

Vedel, H. and Lange, J. *Trees and Bushes in Wood and Hedgerow*, adapted by H.L. Edlin, Methuen, London 1960

Acknowledgments

All photographic illustration by M. Nimmo except the following:
H. Edlin: 6, 7, 8, 12 left, 22 top, 33 bottom, 37, 41, 57 top, 59. Bavestrelli, Bevilacqua and Prato: 19, 28, 36, 92, 106, 109 top. Pedone: 26. Marka: 27 bottom left, 113 top. E.P.S.: 57 bottom, 61, 126 top. Paglietta: 94 top.
The publishers acknowledge the help of the Forestry Commission of Great Britain in preparing the drawings which appear in the glossary.